From
Kristen

Christmas 1982

A
WAY
WITH
WORDS

*This book is a lovely idea. It's poems, letters, and
... but ... hymns and prayers, and I think it's
going to be a little joy. God bless you.*

Diana Law
(President of Action for Dysphasic Adults)

A WAY WITH WORDS

FAVOURITE PIECES
chosen by
FAMOUS PEOPLE

Foreword by Jonathan Miller

Edited by Christina Shewell and Virginia Dean

SINCLAIR BROWNE: LONDON

First published 1982 by Sinclair Browne Ltd,
10 Archway Close, London N19 3TD
Second impression 1982

British Library Cataloguing in Publication Data

A Way with words.
  1. English literature
  I. Shewell, Christina　　　II. Dean, Virginia
  820.8　　　　　PR1109

ISBN 0–86300–021–5

Book design by Richard Kelly

Filmset by Northumberland Press Ltd,
Gateshead, Tyne and Wear
Printed in Great Britain by
Richard Clay (The Chaucer Press Ltd), Bungay, Suffolk

We acknowledge with gratitude financial assistance for this project from:

The Bank of England

The British Petroleum Company Ltd

Colchester Speech Group

The Corporation and Members of Lloyd's and Lloyd's Brokers

E. W. Fitch Esq. A.C.I.I.

FOREWORD

This book is an anthology of favourite pieces chosen by people whose professional lives depend on the skilful and persuasive use of words. It is a thanksgiving for the power of speech. To be more accurate it celebrates the gift of language, for speech is not the only form in which language can be expressed. As long as we retain the ability to think in words it doesn't really matter what form these words are uttered in. The deaf can communicate with great verbal subtlety by using manual signs. We can write to one another, wave flags and tap morse buzzers. The medium is relatively unimportant. What matters is the ability to formulate our thoughts as communicable messages. In fact without language it's difficult to imagine how thought itself would be organised. And it's no exaggeration to say that language is not just a medium through which we communicate our thoughts. It's one of the most important methods through which we bring our thoughts into existence.

Through the medium of language we can not only say things about the world – describe it, deplore it and predict it – we can also do things with words. Language enables us to promise, apologise and enter into contracts. The capacity to use language is creative and open-ended, which means that we can utter and understand sentences that we have neither spoken or heard before. To put it another way, language is a competence forever realising itself in original performances, and through the medium of these performances we bring into existence everything that distinguishes us from the animals. What makes this endowment so remarkable is the fact that we can master it in the first five years of life. Here is the most sophisticated achievement of evolution, and yet a mere child can accomplish it. And yet this subtle and amiable skill can be irreversibly damaged by physical injury. Strokes, tumours and accidents can destroy the ability to utter and understand language. And when this happens the resulting dysphasia isolates the victim in a way which is almost unimaginable.

It is important to distinguish dysphasia from some of the other common disorders of speech. It has nothing to do with defects of voice production. In patients who have suffered injury to the tongue or larynx language remains intact, and with re-training it is usually possible to find some alternative way of expressing this competence in a readily understandable material form. But the frustration associated with dysphasia is much more deep seated. What is lost is the ability to conceive the possibility of language. The ability to write may be just as seriously impaired as the ability to talk. And even though the hearing is intact, spoken language may strike the sufferer as incomprehensible gibberish. In recent years clinical techniques for helping such patients have become much more sophisticated, and with the help of speech therapists people who would previously have been lost in a limbo of uncommunicative solitude can be re-introduced to the community of their speaking fellows. This book is dedicated to this unfinished task, and the proceeds will go towards urgently needed funds for supporting further research and treatment.

Jonathan Miller

DANNIE ABSE
POET

They held up a stone.
  I said, 'Stone,'
Smiling they said, 'Stone.'

They showed me a tree.
  I said, 'Tree.'
Smiling they said, 'Tree.'

They shed a man's blood.
  I said, 'Blood.'
Smiling they said, 'Paint.'

They shed a man's blood.
  I said, 'Blood.'
Smiling they said, 'Paint.'

Adapted from the Hebrew of Amir Gilboa

Instead of a comment, I have adapted this poem into English for this anthology.

BRIAN ALDISS
WRITER AND CRITIC

Walking next day upon the fatal shore,
Among the slaughtered bodies of their men
Which the full-stomached sea had cast upon
The sands, it was my unhappy chance to light
Upon a face, whose favour when it lived,
My astonished mind informed me I had seen.
He lay in's armour, as if that had been
His coffin; and the weeping sea, like one
Whose milder temper doth lament the death
Of him whom in his rage he slew, runs up
The shore, embraces him, kisses his cheek,
Goes back again, and forces up the sands
To bury him, and every time it parts
Sheds tears upon him, till at last (as if
It could no longer endure to see the man
Whom it had slain, yet loth to leave him) with
A kind of unresolved unwilling pace,
Winding her waves one in another, like
A man that folds his arms or wrings his hands
For grief, ebbed from the body, and descends
As if it would sink down into the earth,
And hide itself for shame of such a deed.

From: *The Atheist's Tragedy*, by Cyril Tourneur

After England and all but the granite hip of Scotland sank
beneath thermonuclear bombardment, thousands of tattered
human bodies – sodden and hairless as handkerchiefs –
were washed ashore by mighty tidal waves, year after year,
all along the western coasts of Europe, from Narvik and the
Lofoten Islands in the north, from Jutland and the Frisians,
from the rocks of Brittany southward, where the Médoc
grapes grow, driven by furious new currents through Biscay,
to appear informally dressed as Mortality in the charades at
Biarritz and San Sebastian, and along the rainy beaches of
Asturias and Galicia, right down to Lisbon and beyond Cape

St Vincent, where one of the last time-nibbled deliveries of bodies was made as far afield as the estuary of the Guadalquivir, once the private hunting grounds of the Dukes of Medina Sidonia; there, herons, spoonbills, egrets, and birds fresh from nesting places in the permanent snow-caps of the Sierra Nevada gazed like museum-goers on the salt-pickled remains of the inhabitants of Southampton, Scunthorpe and South Ken, who were now part of some greater and more permanent snowcap. Even later than that, sometimes years later, arms still identifiable as arms, or children's hands resembling sleeping crabs, would be cast up in the Azores or on the black laval sands of the Cape Verde islands.

From: *The Eighty Minute Hour*, by Brian Aldiss

This speech comes from Cyril Tourneur's Jacobean play, *The Atheist's Tragedy*. I used to have a passion for the dark plays of Webster and Tourneur, and this splendidly elaborate piece of imagery is one I have admired for many years.

In my 1974 novel *The Eighty-Minute Hour*, I imitated it, though I suppose no one but me would ever recognise the relationship between the two pieces.

THOMAS ALLEN
SINGER

The long, long road over the moors and up into the forest
– who trod it into being first of all? Man, a human being, the
first that came here. There was no path before he came. Afterwards, some beast or other, following the faint tracks over
marsh and moorland, wearing them deeper; after these again
some Lapp gained scent of the path, and took that way from
field to field, looking to his reindeer. Thus was made the road
through the great Almenning – the common tracts without
an owner; no-man's land.

The man comes, walking towards the north. He bears a
sack, the first sack, carrying food and some few implements.
A strong, coarse fellow, with a red iron beard, and little scars
on face and hands; sites of old wounds – were they gained
in toil or fight? Maybe the man has been in prison, and is
looking for a place to hide; or a philosopher, maybe, in search
of peace. This or that, he comes: the figure of a man in this
great solitude. He trudges on; bird and beast are silent all
about him; now and again he utters a word or two; speaking
to himself. 'Eyah – well, well' – so he speaks to himself. Here
and there, where the moors give place to a kindlier spot, an
open space in the midst of the forest, he lays down the sack
and goes exploring; after a while he returns, heaves the sack
to his shoulder again, and trudges on. So through the day,
noting time by the sun; night falls, and he throws himself
down on the heather, resting on one arm.

From: *The Growth of the Soil*, by Knut Hamsun

I love Norway – my North Eastern childhood/heritage being partly
responsible I suspect.

The character in this story could be Hamsun himself. Possess-
ing a few basic materials, he builds his home and begins his
'growth'.

I admire, rather envy this quality, particularly in our materialistic
age, but even more do I enjoy Hamsun's evocative description of
a heathery landscape and the immediately endearing quality of the
character, perhaps because we are instantly aware that this man is
in total harmony with his surroundings – a truly enviable position.

JOHN ARLOTT

WRITER AND BROADCASTER

Here the horse-mushrooms make a fairy ring,
  Some standing upright and some overthrown,
A small Stonehenge, where heavy black snails cling
  And bite away, like Time, the tender stone.

From: *The White Blackbird*, by Andrew Young

It was November 1941; the air raid alarm had sounded. In the incident control room in the centre of Southampton – constantly bombed during the war – every pen, paper and desk was ready for action; so, there was nothing to do until the bombs fell. Nothing, that is, except read.

After many months of searching out material for a collection of topographical verse, I had become an on-sight critic of descriptive writing. Andrew Young, it seemed, might offer some good material. The book was *The White Blackbird*: prospecting, skimming rather than reading; reaching the last page and pausing – only those four lines.

In that moment I – and here 'knew' is not the word, nor 'understood' no one knows, nor understands poetry – I *felt* what poetry is; the difference between it and verse. It might have happened elsewhere in the same book; in many another book, by many another poet. It happened to happen in that poem in Andrew Young's book. It led to a meeting, an increasingly deep appreciation of his work; and a friendship that endured until his death. Above all, it enriched reading – and, indeed, life itself – from that night onward. Soon afterwards the bombs fell. The work was done efficiently enough; but with the realisation of experience permeating the back of the mind.

PROF. SIR ALFRED AYER
PHILOSOPHER

I wish to propose for the reader's favourable consideration a doctrine which may, I fear, appear wildly paradoxical and subversive. The doctrine in question is this: that it is undesirable to believe a proposition when there is no ground whatever for supposing it true. I must, of course, admit that if such an opinion became common it would completely transform our social life and our political system; since both are at present faultless, this must weigh against it. I am also aware (what is more serious) that it would tend to diminish the incomes of clairvoyants, bookmakers, bishops and others who have done nothing to deserve good fortune here or hereafter. In spite of these grave arguments, I maintain that a case can be made out for my paradox, and I shall try to set it forth.

From: *Sceptical Essays*, by Bertrand Russell

This is the opening paragraph of Bertrand Russell's *Sceptical Essays*, which was published in 1928. It was the first work of modern philosophy that I read, and set a standard to which I have aspired throughout my professional career.

SIR DOUGLAS BADER
AVIATOR

For I dipt into the future, far as human eye could see,
Saw the Vision of the world, and all the wonder that would
be;
Saw the heavens fill with commerce, argosies of magic sails,
Pilots of the purple twilight, dropping down with costly bales;
Heard the heavens fill with shouting, and there rain'd a
ghastly dew
From the nations' airy navies grappling in the central blue.

From: 'Locksley Hall', by Alfred Lord Tennyson

All my life I have been a reader of poetry and have enjoyed it. This
fascinatingly prophetic poem was written by Alfred Tennyson in
1837, when he was 28 years old. Like one other poem I know, this
is a complete prophecy, if not virtually a description, of the Battle
of Britain which occurred 103 years later (in 1940). '. . . the heavens
fill with shouting,' refers to radio-telephonic communications
between pilots. It is significant when one reads such prophecies (not
related to the New Testament) after the event and finds them so
accurate.

KENNETH BAKER
MP

Dim dawn behind the tamarisks – the sky is saffron-yellow –
   As the women in the village grind the corn,
And the parrots seek the river-side, each calling to his fellow
   That the Day, the staring Eastern Day, is born.
     O the white dust on the highway! O the stenches in the
       byway!
     O the clammy fog that hovers over earth!
    And at Home they're making merry 'neath the white and
      scarlet berry –
     What part have India's exiles in their mirth?

Full day behind the tamarisks – the sky is blue and
      staring –
   As the cattle crawl afield beneath the yoke,
And they bear One o'er the field-path, who is past all hope
     or caring,
   To the ghat below the curling wreaths of smoke.
     Call on Rama, going slowly, as ye bear a brother lowly –
      Call on Rama – he may hear, perhaps, your voice!
    With our hymn-books and our psalters we appeal to
      other altars,
     And to-day we bid 'good Christian men rejoice!'

High noon behind the tamarisks – the sun is hot above us –
   As at Home the Christmas Day is breaking wan.
They will drink our healths at dinner – those who tell us how
     they love us,
   And forget us till another year be gone!
     O the toil that knows no breaking! O the *heimweh*,
      ceaseless, aching!
     O the black dividing Sea and alien Plain!
    Youth was cheap – wherefore we sold it. Gold was
      good – we hoped to hold it.
     And to-day we know the fulness of our gain!

Grey dusk behind the tamarisks – the parrots fly together –
  As the Sun is sinking slowly over Home;
And his last ray seems to mock us shackled in a lifelong
       tether
  That drags us back howe'er so far we roam.
    Hard her service, poor her payment – she in
        ancient, tattered raiment –
      India, she the grim Stepmother of our kind.
    If a year of life be lent her, if her temple's shrine we
      enter,
    The door is shut – we may not look behind.

Black night behind the tamarisks – the owls begin their
       chorus –
  As the conches from the temple scream and bray.
With the fruitless years behind us and the hopeless years
       before us,
  Let us honour, O my brothers, Christmas Day!
    Call a truce, then, to our labours – let us feast with
       friends and neighbours,
    And be merry as the custom of our caste;
  For, if faint and forced the laughter, and if sadness
       follow after,
  We are richer by one mocking Christmas past.

     From: *Christmas in India*, by Rudyard Kipling

Kipling lived and worked as a young journalist in India for only
7 years. But during that time, the richness and variety of Indian
culture and life burnt into his imagination just as brightly as the
Indian sun burnt down on the dusty plains. The British Government of India was a miracle of organisation and dedication and Kipling was the poetic genius who captured it for all time.
  A very small number of administrators, lawyers, engineers,
soldiers, teachers and missionaries ran a vast and diverse country
with tens of millions of people. The empire builders did many
mundane but necessary things like building roads, laying railways,
providing water supplies, administering justice and creating
schools: generally shouldering other men's burdens. Few went to
India in Victorian times to make money; as Kipling says, 'Hard her
service, poor her payment'. They were often rewarded by fever,

loneliness, disease and death. The old colonial cemetery in Calcutta with its crumbling tombstones is full of young British men and women who died in their twenties and thirties. Walking through it, you cannot help being filled with sadness and pride.

In this poem, Kipling captures these two feelings. The exiles spend another long hot day in India while their forgetful friends back home celebrate Christmas. There is nostalgia for the merriness of the festivities, for the holly and the mistletoe, but this mingles with an almost tragic irony: for while nostalgia pulls them back, the hard demands of service, service to India and to their own sense of duty holds them fast in a foreign land.

JOAN BAKEWELL
WRITER & BROADCASTER

The set for Act 1 of *La Vestale* consisted of a platform laid over the stage, raised about a foot at the back and sloping evenly to the footlights. This was meant to represent the interior of the Temple where burned the sacred flame, and had therefore to look like marble; the designer had achieved a convincing alternative by covering the raised stage in Formica. But the Formica was slippery; to avoid the risk of a performer taking a tumble, designer and stage manager had between them discovered that an ample sprinkling of lemon juice would make the surface sufficiently sticky to provide a secure foothold. The story now forks; down one road, there lies the belief that the member of the stage staff whose duty it was to sprinkle the lifesaving liquid, and who had done so without fail at rehearsal and at the earlier performances (this was the last one of the Festival), had simply forgotten. Down the other branch in the road is a much more attractive rumour: that the theatre charlady, inspecting the premises in the afternoon, had seen to her horror and indignation that the stage was covered in the remains of some spilt liquid, and, inspired by professional pride, had thereupon set to and given it a good scrub and polish all over.

The roads now join again, for apart from the superior charm of the second version, it makes no difference what the explanation was. What matters is what happened.

What happened began to happen very early. The hero of the opera strides on to the stage immediately after the curtain has gone up. The hero strode; and instantly fell flat on his back. There was a murmur of sympathy and concern from the audience for his embarrassment and for the possibility that he might have been hurt; it was the last such sound that was to be heard that night, and it was very soon to be replaced by sounds of a very different nature.

The hero got to his feet, with considerable difficulty, and, having slid some way down the stage in falling, proceeded to stride up-stage to where he should have been in the first place; he had, of course, gone on singing throughout, for the music had not stopped. Striding up-stage, however, was plainly more difficult than he had reckoned on, for every time he took a step and tried to follow it with another, the foot with which he had taken the first proceeded to slide down-stage again, swiftly followed by its companion; he may not have known it, but he was giving a perfect demonstration of what is called *marcher sur place*, a graceful manoeuvre normally used in mime, and seen at its best in the work of Marcel Marceau.

Finding progress uphill difficult, indeed impossible, the hero wisely decided to abandon the attempt to stay where he was, singing bravely on, no doubt calculating that, since the stage was brightly lit, the next character to enter would notice him and adjust his own movements accordingly. So it proved, in a sense at least, for the next character to enter was the hero's trusted friend and confidant, who, seeing his hero further down-stage than he was supposed to be, loyally decided to join him there. Truth to tell, he had little choice, for from the moment he had stepped on to the stage he had begun to slide downhill, arms semaphoring, like Scrooge's clerk on the way home to his Christmas dinner. His downhill progress was arrested by his fetching up against his friend with a thud; this, as it happened, was not altogether inappropriate, as the opera called for them to embrace in friendly greeting at that point. It did not, however, call for them, locked in each other's arms and propelled by the impetus of the friend's descent, to career helplessly further down-stage with the evident intention of going straight into the orchestra pit with vocal accompaniment – for the hero's aria had, on the arrival of his companion, been transformed into a duet.

On the brink of ultimate disaster they managed to arrest their joint progress to destruction and, working their way along the edge of the stage like mountaineers seeking a route round an unbridgeable crevasse, most gallantly began, with infinite pain and by a form of progress most aptly described in the title of Lenin's famous pamphlet, *Four Steps Forward, Three Steps Back*, to climb up the terrible hill. It speedily became clear that this hazardous ascent was not being made simply from a desire to retain dramatic credibility; it had a much more practical object. The only structure breaking the otherwise all too smooth surface of the stage was a marble pillar, a yard or so high, on which there burned the sacred flame of the rite. This pillar was embedded firmly in the stage, and it had obviously occurred to both mountaineers at once that if they could only reach it it would provide a secure base for their subsequent operations, since if they held on to it for dear life they would at any rate be safe from any further danger of sliding downhill and/or breaking their necks.

It was soon borne in upon them that they had undertaken a labour of truly Sisyphean proportions, and would have been most heartily pardoned by the audience if they had abandoned the librettist's words at this point, and fitted to the music instead the old moral verse:

> The heights by great men reached and kept,
> Were not attained by sudden flight;
> But they, while their companions slept,
> Were toiling upwards in the night.

By this time the audience – all 440 of us – were in a state of such abandon with laughter that several of us felt that if this were to continue a moment longer we would be in danger of doing ourselves a serious internal mischief; little did we know that the fun was just beginning, for shortly after Mallory and Irvine reached their longed-for goal, the chorus entered, and instantly flung themselves *en masse* into a very freely choreographed version of *Les Patineurs*, albeit to the wrong music. The heroine herself, the priestess Giulia, with a survival instinct strong enough to suggest that she would be the one to get close to should any reader of these lines happen to be shipwrecked along with the Wexford opera company, skated into the wings and kicked her shoes off and then, finding on her return that this had hardly improved matters, skated back to the wings and removed her tights as well.

Now, however, the singing never having stopped for a moment, the chorus had come to the same conclusion as had the hero and his friend, namely that holding on to the holy pillar was the only way to remain upright and more or less immobile. The trouble with this conclusion was that there was only one such pillar on the stage, and it was a small one; as the cast crowded round it, it seemed that there would be some very unseemly brawling among those seeking a handhold, a foothold, even a bare finger-hold, on this tiny island of security in the terrible sea of impermanence. By an instinctive understanding of the principles of co-operation, however, they decided the matter without bloodshed; those nearest the pillar clutched it, those next nearest clutched the clutchers, those farther away still clutched those, and so on until, in a kind of daisy-chain that snaked across the stage, everybody was accommodated.

The condition of the audience was now one of fully extended hysteria, which was having the most extraordinary effect – itself intensifying the audience's condition – on the orchestra. At Wexford, the orchestra pit runs under the stage; only a single row of players – those at the edge of the pit nearest the audience, together, of course, with the conductor – could see what was happening on the stage. The rest realised that *something* out of the ordinary was going on up there, and would have been singularly dull of wit if they had not, for many members of the audience were now slumped on the floor weeping helplessly in the agony of their mirth, and although the orchestra at Wexford cannot see the stage, it can certainly see the auditorium.

Theologians tell us that the delights of the next world are eternal. Perhaps; but what is certain is that all earthly ones, alas, are temporary, and duly, after giving us a glimpse of the more enduring joy of Heaven that must have strengthened the devout in their faith and caused instant conversion among many of the unbelievers, the entertainment came to an end when the first act of the opera did so, amid such cheering as I had never before heard in an opera house, and can never hope to hear again. In the interval before Act II, a member of the production staff walked back and forth across the stage, sprinkling it with the precious nectar, and we knew that our happiness was at an end. But he who, after such happiness, would have demanded more, would be greedy indeed, and most of us were content to know that, for one crowded half-hour, we on honeydew had fed, and drunk the milk of Paradise.

From: *Conducted Tour*, by Bernard Levin

It's always important that those who love opera can laugh at it too. Bernard Levin does both.

GENERAL SIR HUGH BEACH
WARDEN, ST GEORGE'S HOUSE, WINDSOR CASTLE

It is interesting to contemplate a tangled bank, clothed with many plants of many kinds, with birds singing on the bushes, with various insects flitting about, and with worms crawling through the damp earth, and to reflect that these elaborately constructed forms, so different from each other, and dependent upon each other in so complex a manner, have all been produced by laws acting around us. These laws, taken in the largest sense, being Growth with Reproduction; Inheritance which is almost implied by reproduction; Variability from the indirect and direct action of the conditions of life, and from use and disuse: a Ratio of Increase so high as to lead to a Struggle for Life, and as a consequence to Natural Selection, entailing Divergence of Character and the Extinction of less-improved forms. Thus, from the war of nature, from famine and death, the most exalted object which we are capable of conceiving, namely, the production of the higher animals, directly follows. There is grandeur in this view of life, with its several powers, having been originally breathed by the Creator into a few forms or into one; and that, whilst this planet has gone cycling on according to the fixed law of gravity, from so simple a beginning endless forms most beautiful and most wonderful have been, and are being evolved.

From: *The Origin of Species*, by Charles Darwin

This famous passage is the final paragraph of *The Origin of Species by means of natural selection or the preservation of favoured races in the struggle for life*, which was published in 1859 and written by Charles Darwin over the preceding fifteen years. It summarises the principal argument of the book, which succeeded for the first time in giving a comprehensible account of the process of evolution.

The passage has many interesting features. The opening sentence speaks of Darwin the naturalist; and it was indeed on his astonishing powers of observation, as much as on his power of reasoning that his reputation rests. The mechanisms by which what he called Variability (and is now called mutation) actually takes place were hardly at all understood in his time. Ironically a vital piece of evidence, in the shape of the original paper by Gregor Mendel, was in Darwin's possession but at his death the pages were still uncut. But while the details of the process remain highly contentious the essence of Darwin's thesis has largely stood the test of time. In the final sentence Darwin speaks of the Creator. It is by no means clear that at the time of writing Darwin still believed in the Christian God as his Victorian contemporaries understood Him, but it is difficult not to be touched by the vision of grandeur in creation as it commended itself to one of the most radically creative minds of his day.

TONY BENN M.P.
SOCIALIST

We, the free People of England, to whom God hath given
hearts, means and opportunity to effect the same, do with
submission to his wisdom, in his name, and desiring the
equity thereof may be to his praise and glory; Agree to
ascertain our Government to abolish all arbitrary Power, and
to set bounds and limits both to our Supreme, and all Sub-
ordinate Authority, and remove all known Grievances. And
accordingly do declare and publish to all the world, that we
are agreed as followeth,

That the Supreme Authority of England and the Terri-
tories therewith incorporate, shall be and reside hence-
forth in a Representative of the people consisting of four
hundred persons, but no more; in the choice of whom
(according to natural right) all men of the age of one and
twenty years and upwards (not being servants, or receiv-
ing alms, or having served the late King in Arms or
voluntary Contributions), shall have their voices.

From: the preamble to the third draft of *The Agreement
of the People*, drawn up by The Levellers, 1 May 1649

The Levellers held themselves to be free-born Englishmen,
entitled to the protection of a natural law of human rights which
they believed to originate in the will of God, rights vested in the
people to whom alone true sovereignty belonged. These sovereign
rights, the Levellers maintained, were only loaned to Parliament,
who, having been elected on a wide popular franchise, would hold
them in trust. The Levellers also believed passionately in religious
toleration and rejected oppression by presbyters as much as by
priests, wishing to end the horrific record of executions, burnings,
brandings and banishments that Christians had perpetrated on
themselves and others, that had led to the martyrdom of thousands
of good Catholics and Protestants, dissenters, Jews and gentiles
alike.

The rank and file within the New Model Army spoke through
Adjutants, Agents or Agitators (hence the special odium attaching
to that word in the British establishment to this day) who wore the

sea-green colours that are still associated with incorruptibility. They demanded and won – for a time – democratic control of the Armed Forces and secured equal representation on a Grand Council of the Army, sharing decisions with the generals and colonels, known to them as the Grandees. They regarded the Normans as oppressors of England and the King as the symbol of that Conquest who was buttressed and supported by land-owners who had seized much land once held in common, land that they argued should be restored to common ownership.

They argued for universal state schools and hospitals to be provided at public expense three centuries before our generation began, so painfully, to construct the Welfare State, the National Health Service and the comprehensive school system against so much resistance.

The Levellers distilled their political philosophy by discussion out of their own experience, mixing theory and practice, thought and action, and by doing so they passed on to succeeding generations a formula for social progress from which we can learn how to tackle the problems of our time. The Levellers won wide support among the people as a whole; and though Cromwell and his generals ultimately defeated them, their ideas still retain a special place in the political traditions of the people of England.

Looking back on these ideas from the vantage point of the present, and knowing that they came out of the minds and experience of working people, few of whom enjoyed the formal education available today, we can imagine the intense excitement and the controversy that those demands must have created when they were first formulated. It is also a real comfort for us to discover that, in our present social, political, human and industrial struggles, we are the inheritors of such a strong and ancient tradition of action and analysis.

My commentary first appeared in my *Arguments for Socialism*. I chose the piece because it still seems to be a message for our times.

JOHN BERGER
WRITER

I went into my father's curragh and Tomás into his. I was very happy, looking down into the sea and listening to the glug-glag of the water against the boat. After a while I put out an oar and I was dipping it gently when somehow I gave it a pull. The curragh gave a leap and her bow struck a rock, the way the two men who were standing on the thwarts, boarding the nets, were thrown down. 'Your soul to the devil, what have you done?' cried Shaun Tomás who was near me. He caught me by the head and heels as if to throw me overboard. When I saw the sea below me I screamed, thinking he was in earnest, but he drew me in again quickly. After that I stayed as quiet as a cat and my heart beating like a bird you would have in your hand.

Some of the curraghs were leaving now, moving out west through the mouth of the Strand. When my father was ready they put me out of the curragh and she moved away. I walked up to the top of the slip. There I met Tomás.

'Do you know where we will go now?' said he. 'Back to the top of the Strand and we will have a great view of the curraghs fishing.'

There was not an old woman in the village but was already there, sitting on her haunches looking out at the curraghs. The evening was very still. It was a fine sight to look out towards the shore of Yellow Island at the shoals of mackerel and the curraghs running round on them like big black flies.

There was no understanding the old women now, who were foaming at the mouth with their roaring.

'Your soul to the devil,' cried one to her husband, 'throw the head of your net behind them!'

'Musha, you're my love for ever, Diarmid!' cried another when she saw her husband making a fine haul of fish.

One woman, Kate O'Shea, her hair streaming in the wind like a mad woman's, was screaming:

'The devil take you, Tigue, draw in your nets and go west to the south of the Sound where you will get fish for the souls of the dead. Och, my pity to be married to you, you good-for-nothing!'

'May the yellow devil carry ye away, ye have the place destroyed with your noise!' shouted one of the fishermen when he heard the screams ashore.

As for Tomás and me, our hearts were black with laughing at the old women, their shawls thrown off, waving their arms at their husbands, calling to them to come here and to come there around the fish, until the fish themselves seemed to be distracted by them.

The sea was now like a pane of glass. You could hear the mackerel splashing in the nets and others out of their senses rushing across the top of the water in an effort to escape, for the day was strong yet and they could see the nets.

. Before long Shaun Fada came down from the village, and with him Shaun Michael and the Púncán.[1] They stood in the middle of the crowd watching the women.

'Achván, achván,[2] aren't they the mad crowd?' says Shaun Michael.

'They are, musha, so,' agrees the Púncán, throwing out a big spittle of tobacco.

'By the devil's body, is it going out of your wits you are?' cries Shaun Fada to the women.

'Arra, your soul to the devil, my lad, what's on you?' says old Mickil, stretched out on the grass.

'What's on me is a pain in my head listening to those seal-cows of women.'

'Och, the devil himself couldn't get right from some of them!'

The women were growing hoarse now, especially Kate O'Shea.

'Kate is giving out,' says Shaun Michael.

'The devil a wonder, short of her having a throat of iron,' says Shaun Fada.

'Faith,' says old Mickil, rising up on his elbow, 'I am here for half an hour now and you wouldn't find a bull-seal to bellow the like of her ever since.'

'Look,' says Tomás to me, 'your father is drawing in his net again.'

The din stopped. Not a word from anyone. You would think a hand had been laid on every mouth, everyone watching my father drawing the nets. He caught hold of one end of them.

'Musha,' said Shaun Michael, 'I think the net is straight down with fish.'

At that my heart rose with delight. My father drew in the end of the net. There was a mackerel in every mesh.

[1] Nickname of old man in the Island.
[2] Old phrase, said to mean 'By the white steed'.

From: *Twenty Years a-Growing*, by Maurice O'Sullivan

From this marvellous and yet insufficiently read book, I might have chosen a hundred quotations. All its pages are about learning from life. Close to. At first hand. In the timelessness of childhood with all its enthusiasm and all its fears. Life lived at that proximity demands to be told as a story. Everything is story and everything is real. And all the stories are a tribute to the truthfulness of a way of life, however harsh; and a tribute to the courage of the Irish, among the most maltreated peoples in modern history.

SIR JOHN BETJEMAN
POET LAUREATE

I remember, I remember,
The house where I was born.
The little window where the sun
Came peeping through at morn;
He never came a wink too soon,
Nor brought too long a day,
But now, I often wish the night
Had borne my breath away!

I remember, I remember,
The roses red and white,
The vi'lets, and the lily-cups,
Those flowers made of light!
The lilacs where the robin built,
And where my brother set
The laburnam on his birthday, –
The tree is living yet!

I remember, I remember
Where I was used to swing,
And thought the air must rush as fresh
To swallows on the wing:
My spirits flew in feathers then,
That is so heavy now,
And summer pools could hardly cool,
The fever on my brow!

I remember, I remember
The fir trees dark and high;
I used to think their slender tops
Were close against the sky:
It was a childish ignorance,
But now 'tis little joy
To know I'm farther off from heav'n
Than when I was a boy.

I remember, I remember by Thomas Hood

The melancholy of this poem is exactly suited to my mood today and every day. It is simple, clear and can be heard by the inner ear like a sad, far, bell.

ROBERT BOLT
WRITER

The peace of afternoon had fallen upon the world one day towards the end of Constable Plimmer's second week of the simple life, when his attention was attracted by a whistle. It was followed by a musical 'Hi!'

Constable Plimmer looked up. On the kitchen balcony of a second-floor flat a girl was standing. As he took her in with a slow and exhaustive gaze, he was aware of strange thrills. There was something about this girl which excited Constable Plimmer. I do not say that she was a beauty; I do not claim that you or I would have raved about her; I merely say that Constable Plimmer thought she was All Right.

'Miss?' he said.

'Got the time about you?' said the girl. 'All the clocks have stopped.'

'The time,' said Constable Plimmer, consulting his watch, 'wants exactly ten minutes to four'.

'Thanks.'

'Not at all, miss.'

The girl was inclined for conversation. It was that gracious hour of the day when you have cleared lunch and haven't got to think of dinner yet, and have a bit of time to draw a breath or two. She leaned over the balcony and smiled pleasantly.

'If you want to know the time, ask a pleeceman,' she said. 'You been on this beat long?'

'Just short of two weeks, miss.'

'I been here three days.'

'I hope you like it, miss.'

'So-so. The milkman's a nice boy.'

Constable Plimmer did not reply. He was busy, silently hating the milkman. He knew him – one of those good-looking blighters; one of those oiled and curled perishers; one of those blooming fascinators who go about the world making things hard for ugly, honest men with loving hearts. Oh, yes, he knew the milkman.

'He's a rare one with his jokes,' said the girl.

Constable Plimmer went on not replying. He was perfectly aware that the milkman was a rare one with his jokes. He had heard him. The way girls fell for anyone with the gift of the gab – that was what embittered Constable Plimmer.

'He –' she giggled. 'He calls me Little Pansy-Face'.

'If you'll excuse me, miss,' said Constable Plimmer coldly, 'I'll have to be getting along on my beat.'

Little Pansy-Face! And you couldn't arrest him for it! What a world! Constable Plimmer paced upon his way, a blue-clad volcano.

It is a terrible thing to be obsessed by a milkman. To Constable Plimmer's disordered imagination it seemed that, dating from this interview, the world became one solid milkman. Wherever he went, he seemed to run into this milkman. If he was in the front road, this milkman – Alf Brooks, it appeared, was his loathsome name – came rattling past with his jingling cans as if he were Apollo driving his chariot. If he was round at the back, there was Alf, his damned tenor doing duets with the balconies. And all this in defiance of the known law of natural history that milkmen do not come out after five in the morning. This irritated Constable Plimmer. You talk of a man 'going home with the milk' when you mean that he sneaks in in the small hours of the morning. If all milkmen were like Alf Brooks the phrase was meaningless.

He brooded. The unfairness of Fate was souring him. A man expects trouble in his affairs of the heart from soldiers and sailors, and to be cut out by even a postman is to fall before a worthy foe; but milkmen – no! Only grocers' assistants and telegraph-boys were intended by Providence to fear milkmen.

Yet here was Alf Brooks, contrary to all rules, the established pet of the mansions. Bright eyes shone from balconies when his 'Milk – oo – oo' sounded. Golden voices giggled delightedly at his bellowed chaff. And Ellen Brown, whom he called Little Pansy-Face, was definitely in love with him.

They were keeping company. They were walking out. This crushing truth Edward Plimmer learned from Ellen herself.

She had slipped out to mail a letter at the pillar-box on the corner, and she reached it just as the policeman arrived there in the course of his patrol.

Nervousness impelled Constable Plimmer to be arch. ''Ullo, 'ullo, 'ullo,' he said. 'Posting love-letters?'

From: 'The Romance of an Ugly Policeman', in *The Man With Two Left Feet*, by P. G. Wodehouse

I walked up and down my bookcases, wondering what I should choose when I came upon a serried row of P. G. Wodehouse. Then it flashed upon me that a morning swallow of the Master of wit was all that I could take during my late illness. Biography, History, Novels, and Politics were all beyond me. So I have chosen 'The Romance of an Ugly Policeman'.

MICHAEL BOND
WRITER

After dinner I sat and waited for Pyle in my room over the rue Catinat; he had said, 'I'll be with you at latest by ten,' and when midnight struck I couldn't stay quiet any longer and went down into the street. A lot of old women in black trousers squatted on the landing: it was February and I suppose too hot for them in bed. One trishaw driver pedalled slowly by towards the river-front and I could see lamps burning where they had disembarked the new American planes. There was no sign of Pyle anywhere in the long street.

From: *The Quiet American*, by Graham Greene

For me, one of the hardest parts about writing is always the opening paragraph. It's the part I worry about and lose the most sleep over; until it's right I can't get started.

The same applies to a lesser extent to the closing paragraph; except that by then, for better or worse, it's all over and you have finished.

With the former you have to catch the reader's attention, exciting their interest so that they will want to read on. With the latter you need to make them feel it was all worth while.

The bit in between is often hard work – a bit like hill climbing, you reach one peak only to find another one ahead of you, then another, but you almost always get there in the end.

Perhaps one day someone will compile a collection of opening paragraphs. If they do then one writer assured of a place is Graham Greene, who is a master of the art of catching one's attention and setting the scene in a few well-chosen words, as he does here at the start of 'The Quiet American'.

ROB BUCKMAN
DOCTOR AND BROADCASTER

It is only recently that science has found out the exact structure of the tiny cell formations which go to make up life. Only yesterday, in fact.

Every higher animal starts life as a single cell. This much is obvious. Look at the rainbow. Look at the formation of frost on the window pane. Don't look now. Wait a minute ... Now look.

This cell measures no more than 1/125 of an inch in diameter at first, but you mustn't be discouraged. It looks like nothing at all, even under the strongest microscope, and, before we knew just how important they were, they were often thrown away. We now know that if it were not for these tiny, tiny cells, we should none of us be here to-day. This may or may not be a recommendation for the cells. *Quien sabe?*

Shortly after the cell decides to go ahead with the thing, it gets lonely and divides itself up into three similar cells, just for company's sake and to have someone to talk to. They soon find out that they aren't particularly congenial, so they keep on dividing themselves up into other cells until there is a regular mob of them. Then they elect an entertainment committee and give a show.

After the show, there is a fight, and the thing breaks up into different cliques or groups. One group think they are white corpuscles or *phagocytes*. Others go around saying that they are *red* corpuscles and to hell with the white.

The other groups of cells devote themselves to music, aesthetic dancing, and the formation of starch which goes into dress shirts. They are all very happy and very busy, and it's nobody's business *what* they do when they aren't working. We certainly are not going to snoop into that here.

We must take up, however, the work of the brain cells, as it is in the brain that the average man of to-day does his thinking. (Aha-ha-ha-ha-ha-ha!)

Oh, let's *not* take up the brain cells. You know as much about them as anybody does, and what's the use anyway? Suppose you *do* learn something to-day. You're likely to die to-morrow, and there you are.

And we *must* go into the question of the size of these cells. That really is important. In about 1/150000 of a cubic inch of blood there are some five million cells afloat. This is, as you will see, about the population of the City of London, except that the cells don't wear any hats. Thus, in our whole body, there are perhaps (six times seven is forty-two, five times eight is forty, put down nought and carry your four, eight times nine is seventy-two and four is seventy-six, put down six and carry your seven and then, adding, six, four, three, one, six, nought, nought, nought), oh, about a billion or so of these red corpuscles alone, not counting overhead and breakage. In the course of time, that runs into figures.

Now when it comes to reproduction, you have to look out. In the cuttlefish, for example, there is what is known as 'greesion' or budding. The organism as a whole remains un-altered, except that one small portion of it breaks off and goes into business for itself. This, of course, makes a very pretty picture, but gets nowhere. In the case of multicellular animals, like the orange, it results in a frightful confusion.

We should have said that there are two classes of animals, unicellular and multicellular. From the unicellular group we get our coal, iron, wheat and ice, and from the multicellular our salt, pepper, chutney and that beautiful silk dress which milady wears so proudly. Woollen and leather goods we import.

You will see then that by grafting a piece of one species on another species, you can mix the cells and have all kinds of fun. Winkler, in 1902, grafted a piece of Solanum (the genus to which the potato belongs) on to a stock of another kind, and then, after the union had been established, cut the stem across, just at the point of junction. The bud was formed of the intermingled tissues of the two species and was most peculiar looking.

Winkler was arrested.

From: *Cell-formations and their work*, by Robert Benchley

Being serious about humour is a bit of a waste of time. In fact some people believe that all critical appraisal is totally useless, and that critical appraisal of humour is doubly totally useless. This is because if a joke doesn't happen to make you laugh, that is the end of it and nothing can be done about it. Explaining the psychology underpinning a dud joke is never a resuscitation, it can only be a post-mortem. As a matter of fact, Sigmund Freud demonstrated this when he wrote a great long book about intricate German puns which could only be understood by those with an intimate working knowledge of naval history, differential calculus, Bavarian agriculture and Viennese army slang. Many modern psychologists believe that this is why Freud never made it as a stand-up comedian. Certainly, it was enough to stop me from ever trying to explain a joke.

Another reason for my being so shy about this introduction is that there is nothing that dampens the sense of humour quite as much as a warm recommendation. Nothing puts me off a funny book as quickly as someone telling me that they never normally laugh out loud at books but reading this one on the train, no word of a lie, they were laughing and snorting, and snickering and rolling around so much that they were eventually thrown off the train by a posse of insurance salesmen just outside Godalming. The moment I hear this, I know that the book will go down like a lead-filled sock. I'll read it with the same riotous hilarity with which I first read *Diagnostic Radiology of the Biliary Tract* by Gerstenblith, Huppert and Dutz – and I never got thrown off a Godalming train reading *that*.

With those two cautions in mind, allow me to present a piece by Robert Benchley. Benchley makes me laugh – in fact I haven't read any author that makes me laugh more. I can't (and won't) say why he makes me laugh, but his style of humour is what is commonly called 'gentle'. Usually when a reviewer calls a humourist 'gentle' he actually means 'not very funny'. Well, Benchley is unlike any other gentle humourist. He's full of ideas, he moves like greased lightning without appearing to hurry and he always seems to be on your side. If you haven't met him before, I'm delighted to be introducing you, and if he doesn't strike even the slightest of sparks with you, I'd be glad to lend you my copy of Gerstenblith, Huppert and Dutz.

ROBERT BURCHFIELD C.B.E.
CHIEF EDITOR OF THE OXFORD DICTIONARIES

When I am animated by this wish, I look with pleasure on my book, however defective, and deliver it to the world with the spirit of a man that has endeavoured well. That it will immediately become popular I have not promised to myself: a few wild blunders, and risible absurdities, from which no work of such multiplicity was ever free, may for a time furnish folly with laughter, and harden ignorance in contempt; but useful diligence will at last prevail, and there never can be wanting some who distinguish desert; who will consider that no dictionary of a living tongue ever can be perfect, since while it is hastening to publication, some words are budding, and some falling away; that a whole life cannot be spent upon syntax and etymology, and that even a whole life would not be sufficient; that he, whose design includes whatever language can express, must often speak of what he does not understand; that a writer will sometimes be hurried by eagerness to the end, and sometimes faint with weariness under a task, which *Scaliger* compares to the labours of the anvil and the mine; that what is obvious is not always known, and what is known is not always present; that sudden fits of inadvertency will surprize vigilance, flight avocations will seduce attention, and casual eclipses will darken learning; and that the writer shall often in vain trace his memory at the moment of need, for that which yesterday he knew with intuitive readiness, and which will come uncalled into his thoughts to-morrow.

From: *Dictionary of the English Language*,
by Samuel Johnson

The Preface to Dr Johnson's Dictionary (1755) is one of the most impressive passages in the English language. This extract, which is the penultimate paragraph of ten tall pages of type, consists of two sentences. It would not be easy to match its surging power and its abiding clarity.

The bushes on the other bank shook and twisted. A trail of movement showed in them, moving quickly from the bank back among the trees. The fire blinked again. Then the flames vanished and a great cloud of white smoke shot up through the green, the base thinned, disappeared, the white cloud rose slowly, turning inside out as it went. Lok leaned foolishly sideways to look round the trees and bushes. The urgency gripped him. He swung himself down the branches till he could see the next tree down river. He leapt at a branch, was on it, and moving like a red squirrel from tree to tree. Then he ran up a trunk again, tore branches away and peered down.

The roar of the fall was a little dulled now and he could see the columns of spray. They brooded over the upper end of the island so that the trees there were obscured. He let his eye run from them down the island to where the bushes had moved and the fire blinked. He could see, though not clearly, into an open space among the trees. The reek from the dead fire still hung over it, slowly dispersing. There were no people in sight but he could see where the bushes had been broken and a track of torn earth made between the shore and the open space. At the inner end of this track, tree-trunks, huge, dead things with the decay of years about them, had gathered themselves together. He inspected the logs, his mouth hanging open and a free hand pressed flat on top of his head. Why should the people bring all this food – he could see the pale fungi clear across the river – and the useless wood with it? They were people without pictures in their heads. Then he saw that there was a dirty smudge in the earth where the fire had been and logs as huge had been used to build it. Without any warning fear flooded into him, fear as complete and unreasoning as Mal's when he had seen the fire burning the forest in his dream. And because he was one of the people, tied to them with a thousand invisible strings, his fear was for the people. He began to quake. The lips writhed back from his teeth, he could not see clearly. He heard his voice crying out through a roaring noise in his ears.

'Ha! Where are you? Where are you?'

Someone thick-legged ran clumsily across the clearing and disappeared. The fire stayed dead and the bushes were combed by a breeze from down river and then were quite still.

Desperately:

'Where are you?'

Lok's ears spoke to Lok.

'?'

So concerned was he with the island that he paid no attention to his ears for a time. He clung swaying gently in the tree-top while the fall grumbled at him and the space on the island remained empty. Then he heard. There were people coming, not on the other side of the water but on this side, far off. They were coming down from the overhang, their steps careless on the stones. He could hear their speech and it made him laugh. The sounds made a picture in his head of interlacing shapes, thin, and complex, voluble and silly, not like the long curve of a hawk's cry, but tangled like line weed on the beach after a storm, muddled as water. This laugh-sound advanced through the trees towards the river. The same sort of laugh-sound began to rise on the island, so that it flitted back and forth across the water. Lok half-fell, half-scrambled down the tree and was on the trail. He ran along it through the ancient smell of the people. The laugh-sound was close by the river bank. Lok reached the place where the log had lain across water. He had to climb a tree, swing and drop down before he was on the trail again. Then among the laugh-sound on this side of the river Liku began to scream. She was not screaming in anger or in fear or in pain, but screaming with that mindless and dreadful panic she might have shown at the slow advance of a snake. Lok spurted, his hair bristling. Need to get at that screaming threw him off the trail and he floundered. The screaming tore him inside. It was not like the screaming of Fa when she was bearing the baby that died, or the mourning of Nil when Mal was buried; it was like the noise the horse makes when the cat sinks its curved teeth into the neck and hangs there, sucking blood. Lok was screaming himself without knowing it and fighting with thorns. And his senses told him through the screaming that Liku was doing what no man and no woman could do. She was moving away across the river.

From: *The Inheritors*, by William Golding

An extraordinary event occurred forty thousand years ago. For two million years human beings had been evolving as hunter-gatherers of increasing skill, culminating in the Neanderthalers – sturdy, intelligent hunters with very large brains who survived appalling climatic changes during an ice age. Then, like a *dénouement* in science fiction, bands of supermen appeared and swept the Neanderthalers aside, as they took over the world in an interval of just a few thousand years, even crossing the sea, which Neanderthalers feared to do. These were our own ancestors, outwardly indistinguishable from highbrowed people who had coexisted unimpressively with the Neanderthalers for a very long time.

A mutation had occurred that suddenly changed the whole style of life on Earth, and set the modern humans on the road to living in cities and flying to the Moon. The most plausible explanation is that fully-fledged language, with the ability to utter and comprehend elaborate sentences, was the leap that made all the difference. It involved rewiring exactly those parts of the brain where injuries cause dysphasia. Archaeologists and neurologists have plenty to say formally about this evolutionary change. But it was one of the most dramatic events in the long history of life on Earth, and the novelist tells it better, when he describes a Neanderthaler encountering the newcomers for the first time, and hearing them speak.

RT HON. JAMES CALLAGHAN
M.P.

Now King Solomon went to Gibeon to offer a sacrifice, for that was the Chief Hill-shrine, and he used to offer a thousand whole-offerings on its altar. There that night the Lord God appeared to him in a dream and said, 'What shall I give you, tell me'. And Solomon answered, 'Thou didst show great and constant love to thy servant David my Father, because he walked before thee in loyalty, righteousness, and integrity of heart, and thou hast maintained this great and constant love towards him and hast now given him a son to succeed him on the throne. Now, O Lord my God, thou hast made thy servant King in place of my father David, though I am a mere child, unskilled in leadership. And I am here in the midst of thy people, the people of thy choice, too many to be numbered or counted. Give thy servant, therefore, a heart with skill to listen, so that he may govern thy people justly and distinguish good from evil. For who is equal to the task of governing this great people of thine.' The Lord was well pleased that Solomon had asked for this, and he said to him, 'Because you have asked for this, and not for long life for yourself, or for wealth, or for the lives of your enemies, but have asked for discernment in administering justice, I grant your request; I give you a heart so wise and so understanding that there has been none like you before your time nor will be after you. I give you furthermore those things for which you did not ask, such wealth and honour as no King of your time can match. And if you conform to my ways and observe my ordinances and commandments, as your father David did, I will give you long life.' Then he awoke, and knew it was a dream.

From: *First Kings, III, 4–15*

I came across this particular extract when I was asked to read the lesson at the Civic Service to inaugurate the new Lord Mayor of Cardiff. It seemed to be particularly appropriate for anyone who is in a position of leadership.

CARMEN CALLIL
PUBLISHER

And the girls who are not married are often getting quite desperate oh yes they are becoming quite desperate, they are saying all the time, it is like the refrain in *The Three Sisters*. It is the *leitmotiv* of all their lives. It is their *Moscow*. Marriage is to them: Oh if we could only go to *Moscow*. Oh if we could only get to *Moscow*. Oh if we could only have got to *Moscow*. By this time it would now already have been all all right.

Oh the sobs and tears and stretching and straining and contriving, and meanwhile the tennis club secretaries have every reason to be pleased, because there is at least always a sub-stratum of subscriptions which are not outstanding, because these silly fatheads will never let their subscriptions get in arrears, oh no, their subscriptions will let them in to *Russia*. At the least it will let them in to the Russia of their matrimonial ambition. Over the frontier at least, if not actually into the suburbs and citadel of Moscow.

From this matrimony of their dreams automatically flow all blessings and benefits. It is for them the *fons et origo*. There is nothing like it. Oh no, dear Reader, there never was anything like the idea these funny asses have of matrimony. And if unfortunately they do pull it off, how unhappy is the situation of the young man who becomes their husband, for sure enough they will very soon discover that marriage is not that *fons et origo*. And then sure enough instead of readjusting their pop-eyed dreams, instead of coming into line with reality, sure enough they will go, they will run mad, but not so excitingly and refreshingly mad as the women of Thebes, they will run mad at their husbands.

From: *Novel on Yellow Paper*, by Stevie Smith

Stevie Smith and Rosamond Lehmann are my two favourite novelists: Rosamond Lehmann because she writes better than any-one about the affliction of being in love, and Stevie Smith because she makes the most fun of the same disease. I haven't chosen a selection from Rosamond Lehmann's work because the best thing to do with her books is to read *all of them*. Stevie, being a poet, lends herself to the wonderful quote. This one makes me laugh a great deal.

JAMES CAMERON
JOURNALIST

Sweetest love, I do not goe,
   For wearinesse of thee,
Nor in hope the world can show
   A fitter Love for mee;
     But since that I
Must dye at last, 'tis best,
To use my selfe in jest
   Thus by fain'd deaths to dye;

Yesternight the Sunne went hence,
   And yet is here to day,
He hath no desire nor sense,
   Nor halfe so short a way:
     Then feare not mee,
But beleeve that I shall make
Speedier journeys, since I take
   More wings and spurres than hee.

O how feeble is mans power,
   That if good fortune fall,
Cannot adde another houre,
   Nor a lost houre recall!
     But come bad chance,
And wee joyne to'it our strength,
And wee teach it art and length,
   It selfe o'er us to'advance.

When thou sigh'st, thou sigh'st not winde,
   But sigh'st my soule away,
When thou weep'st, unkindly kinde,
   My lifes blood doth decay.
     It cannot bee
That thou lov'st mee, as thou say'st,
If in thine my life thou waste,
   Thou are the best of mee.

Let not thy divining heart
  Forethinke me any ill,
Destiny may take thy part,
  And may thy feares fulfill;
    But thinke that wee
Are but turn'd aside to sleepe;
They who one another keepe
  Alive, ne'er parted bee.

'Song', by John Donne

As a retail merchant of words I came long ago to a humility to those who used words as jewels. My affection for John Donne is much derided now; he is defined by the experts as a sentimental old fool, and indeed that is what he may well have been, as am I.

John Donne was a Christian preacher clearly obsessed by the forbidden magic of sex; he redeemed himself from his immensely turgid sermons, which nobody remembers, by slender and delicate erotic verse, which most people do remember.

Certainly I, who came very late to the Elizabethans and who have a simple taste anyhow, found him rewarding. In this 'Sweetest Love' he wrote, though with magic, something I am clumsily stumbling through even now.

BARBARA CARTLAND
WRITER

One thing I know, life can never die,
Translucent, splendid, flaming like the sun,
Only our bodies wither and deny
The life-force when our strength is done.

Let me transmit this wonderful fire,
Even a little through my heart and mind,
Bringing the perfect love we all desire
To those who seek, yet blindly cannot find.

From: *The Light of Love*, by Barbara Cartland

This expresses my faith and the whole wonder and marvel of living.
It is this mystical magnetic Power which pours through us all. It
lets us breathe, think, grow and develop and also makes us
ultimately indestructible and Eternal.

CHARLES CAUSLEY
POET

C'est un trou de verdure où chante une rivière
Accrochant follement aux herbes des haillons
D'argent, où le soleil, de la montagne fière,
Luit; c'est un petit val qui mousse de rayons.

Un soldat jeune, bouche ouverte, tête nue
Et la nuque baignant dans le frais cresson bleu,
Dort: il est étendu dans l'herbe, sous la nue,
Pâle dans son lit vert où la lumière pleut.

Les pieds dans les glaïeuls, il dort. Souriant comme
Sourirait un enfant malade, il fait un somme.
Nature, berce-le chaudement: il a froid!

Les parfums ne font pas frissoner sa narine;
Il dort dans le soleil, la main sur sa poitrine
Tranquille. Il a deux trous rouges au côté droit.

'Le dormeur du val', by Arthur Rimbaud

Couched in a hollow, where a humming stream
Hooks, absently, sun-fragments, silver-white,
And from the proud hill-top beam falls on beam
Laving the valley in a foam of light,

A soldier sleeps, lips parted, bare his head,
His young neck pillowed where blue cresses drown;
He sprawls under a cloud, his truckle-bed
A spread of grass where the gold sky drips down.

His feet drift among reeds. He sleeps alone,
Smiling the pale smile that sick children wear.
Earth, nurse him fiercely! He is cold as stone,
And stilled his senses to the flowering air.

Hand on his breast, awash in the sun's tide
Calmly he sleeps; two red holes in his side.

'Sleeper in the valley' (translation by Charles Causley)

A favourite poem is something one falls in love with. As among
human beings, the precise reasons are often irrational, complicated,
multifarious, difficult to explain. Certainly, in the case of
Rimbaud's *Le dormeur du val*, its strong appeal to me lies far beyond
its qualities of immediacy, the skilful mixture of richness and
simplicity in its language, its musical sound, its subtly dramatic
structure.

Like all masterpieces, it is a living organism, constantly subject
to change; capable of presenting new aspects of its inner life,
revealing fresh secrets, asking yet another question, at each re-
reading. Suffice it, then, for the poem to speak for itself. A number
of English translations already exist, but I wanted to make the piece
an even more intimate part of my imaginative experience by
producing a version of my own.

Rimbaud wrote the poem in 1870, at sixteen. He had first published his verse a year earlier, but forsook writing altogether around
the age of twenty-two and spent the last ten or eleven years of his
life in Africa, often enduring great hardship, as a trader, explorer,
gun-runner, and possibly as a dealer in slaves. He died in Marseilles
in 1891. Society has invariably loved its artistic 'scapegoats' more
than their work. As an extra bonus, I have always enjoyed the
thought that the near-legendary quality of Rimbaud's life has never
for a moment overshadowed the power and originality of his poetry.

JACK CLEMO
POET

But wait! Even I already seem to share
In God's love: what does New Year's hymn declare?
What other meaning do these verses bear?

'All service ranks the same with God:
If now, as formerly He trod
Paradise, His presence fills
Our earth; each only as God wills
Can work, God's puppets, best and worst,
Are we: there is no last nor first.
Say not "a small event": why "small"?
Costs it more pain that this, ye call
A "great event" should come to pass
Than that? Untwine me from the mass
Of deeds which make up life, one deed
Power shall fall short in, or exceed.'

And more of it, and more of it! Oh, yes,
I will pass by and see their happiness,
And envy none, being just as great, no doubt,
Useful to men and dear to God as they.
A pretty thing to care about
So mightily, this single holiday!
But let the sun shine, wherefore repine? –
With thee to lead me, O day of mine,
Down the grass-path grey with dew,
Under the pine-wood blind with boughs,
Where the swallow never flew
As yet, nor cicala dared carouse.

From: 'Pippa Passes', by Robert Browning

These closing lines of Pippa's prologue had a profound influence on me during the formative years of my youth, when I was
seeking a reconciliation between poetic insight and the disturbing
truths of theology. Pippa seemed to affirm a kind of Calvinism, but

it was extremely cheerful, and her vivid girlish charm enabled me to by-pass the grim faces and arid debates of ecclesiastical councils. As she was a Catholic, her use of the word 'puppets' must have been very light-hearted, quite free from the chilly gloom of logical determinism. Here was a poet's Calvinism – a faith which, a few years after Browning wrote the poem, Elizabeth Barrett echoed in one of her love-letters: 'I think how He of the heavens brought us together so wonderfully, holding two souls in His hand'. I was passionately grateful for this vision of a divine purpose in human life and love, especially as most modern poets, narrowed in a wilderness of materialism, had joined the ranks of the 'aimless, helpless, hopeless' drivellers whom Browning castigated in his famous Epilogue to *Asolando*. I was also impressed by the blend of argument and spontaneous response to nature in this passage. The reflections on value-judgments are consoling to people who live restricted and domesticated lives. I often proved the truth of the comment when apparently trivial incidents stirred me to write penetrating poems. The breadth of Browning's sympathies showed me that a joyous acceptance of earthly beauty is not inconsistent with traditional beliefs.

TOM CONTI
ACTOR

I have become so selfish in my grief,
I can no longer mourn the deaths of children,
Memory turned inward,
Like a crouched monkey with a looking glass,
Bright eyed, uncomprehending,
Scans day by day,
The cold grey empty landscape of my love.

Author and title unknown.

To choose ONE of something is always a formidable task. I'm sure it's easier to play King Lear than choose those eight sodding gramophone records. It's like moments when your child having lined up 'Watford', the blue elephant, 'Leonard', the owl, 'Little Leonard', smaller but identical, a white bear, curiously called 'Cesare' – pronounced the Italian way of course – and a wheeled rabbit with the magical name of 'Rabs Fitzrunaway' asks, 'Dada, which one do you like most?'

'Well, of course I like "Rabs-Fitzrunaway" because of his name but "Leonard" is much softer. "Cesare" was given to you on the day of your birth, so ... on and on ...'

'But Dada, just say which one.'

Desperate now, 'Well – I suppose "Cesare".'

'But Dada, don't you think "Leonard" is lovely and cuddly?'

'Yes, I suppose he's a bit softer.'

Pause.

'Some days I like "Watford" best Dada.'

That's it really. 'Some days ...'

Today as I write, men are dying tragically, pointlessly in the seas around the Falkland Islands and I feel bewildered, impotent and angry.

There's no anger in this nor is it a war poem but it contains bewilderment and impotence a plenty. In its economy it delivers a sharp, stunning blow. I'm ashamed to say I don't know who wrote it. I earnestly hope I've remembered it accurately. I found it on a scrap of newspaper, but the author's name was missing.

JILLY COOPER
WRITER

They took Raferty in an ambulance from Great Malvern in order to spare him the jar of the roads. That night he slept in his own spacious loose-box, and the faithful Jim would not leave him that night; he sat up and watched while Raferty slept in so deep a bed of yellow-gold straw that it all but reached to his knees when standing. A last inarticulate tribute to the most gallant horse, the most courteous horse that ever stepped out of stable.

But when the sun came up over Bredon, flooding the breadth of the Severn Valley, touching the slopes of the Malvern Hills that stand opposite Bredon across the valley, gilding the old red bricks of Morton and the weather-vane on its quiet stables, Stephen went into her father's study and she loaded his heavy revolver.

Then they led Raferty out and into the morning; they led him with care to the big north paddock and stood him beside the mighty hedge that had set the seal on his youthful valour. Very still he stood with the sun on his flanks, the groom, Jim, holding the bridle.

Stephen said: 'I'm going to send you away, a long way away, and I've never left you except for a little while since you came when I was a child and you were quite young – but I'm going to send you a long way away because of your pain. Raferty, this is death; and beyond, they say, there's no more suffering.' She paused, then spoke in a voice so low that the groom could not hear her: 'Forgive me, Raferty'.

And Raferty stood there looking at Stephen, and his eyes were so soft as an Irish morning, yet as brave as the eyes that looked into his. Then it seemed to Stephen that he had spoken, that Raferty had said: 'Since to me you are God, what have I to forgive you, Stephen?'

She took a step forward and pressed the revolver high up against Raferty's smooth, grey forehead. She fired, and he dropped to the ground like a stone, lying perfectly still by the mighty hedge that had set the seal on his youthful valour.

From: *The Well of Loneliness*, by Radclyffe Hall

I have always loved horses. I love their dignity, their courage and their beauty. I think one of the most wonderful things in life is the relationship humans can have with animals, for by loving animals we can learn to love each other. Radclyffe Hall is famous for writing a sensational lesbian novel; for this reason few people realise what a good writer she was, as this passage from The Well of Loneliness shows us.

RONNIE CORBETT
COMEDIAN

For the long nights you lay awake
And watched for my unworthy sake:
For your most comfortable hand
That led me through the uneven land:
For all the story-books you read,
For all the pains you comforted,
For all you pitied, all you bore,
In sad and happy days of yore:–
My second Mother, my first Wife,
The angel of my infant life –
From the sick child, now well and old,
Take, nurse, the little book you hold!

And grant it, Heaven, that all who read
May find as dear a nurse at need,
And every child who lists my rhyme,
In the bright fireside, nursery clime,
May hear it in as kind a voice
As made my childish days rejoice!

'To Alison Cunningham, from her boy', dedication from *The
Child's Garden of Verse*, by Robert Louis Stevenson

This poem was written by Robert Louis Stevenson in praise of
the nannie who nursed him as a sick child. I love it as a piece anyway
and I had the pleasure of reading it out at a Children's Service
held in the Cathedral at Christchurch, New Zealand last year. It
was a very moving day in a splendid Cathedral and it was a thrilling
service so I shall always remember the poem. Since I come from
Edinburgh it has particular poignancy for me anyway.

Never was there such a town as ours, I thought, as we fought on the sand-hills with rough boys or dared each other to climb up the scaffolding of half-built houses soon to be called Laburnum or The Beeches. Never was there such a town, I thought, for the smell of fish and chips on Saturday evenings; for the Saturday afternoon cinema matinées where we shouted and hissed our threepences away; for the crowds in the streets with leeks in their hats on international nights; for the park, the inexhaustible and mysterious, bushy Red-Indian hiding park where the hunchback sat alone and the groves were blue with sailors. The memories of childhood have no order, and so I remember that never was there such a dame school as ours, so firm and kind and smelling of galoshes, with the sweet and fumbled music of the piano lessons drifting down from upstairs to the lonely schoolroom, where only the sometimes tearful wicked sat over undone sums, or to repent a little crime – the pulling of a girl's hair during geography, the sly shin-kick under the table during English literature. Behind the school was a narrow lane where only the oldest and boldest threw pebbles at windows, scuffled and boasted, fibbed about their relations:

'My father's got a chauffeur.'

'What's he want a chauffeur for, he hasn't got a car.'

'My father's the richest man in the town.'

'My father's the richest man in Wales.'

'My father owns the world.'

And swopped gob-stoppers for slings, old knives for marbles, kite-string for foreign stamps.

The lane was always the place to tell your secrets, if you did not have any you invented them: occasionally now I dream that I am turning out of school into the lane of confidences when I say to the boys of my class, 'At last, I have a real secret'.

'What is it? What is it?'

'I can fly.'

And when they do not believe me, I flap my arms and slowly leave the ground, only a few inches at first, then gaining air until I fly waving my cap level with the upper windows of the school, peering in until the mistress at the piano screams and the metronome falls to the ground and stops, and there is no more time.

And I fly over the trees and chimneys of my town, over the dockyards skimming the masts and funnels, over Inkerman Street, Sebastopol Street, and the street where all the women wear men's caps, over the trees of the everlasting park, where a brass band shakes the leaves and sends them showering down on to the nurses and the children, the cripples and the idlers, and the gardeners, and the shouting boys: over the yellow seashore, and the stone-chasing dogs, and the old men, and the singing sea.

The memories of childhood have no order, and no end.

From: *Reminiscences of Childhood*, by Dylan Thomas

For me, the town was Holyhead, at the other end of Wales. But it was the same town, with the same cinemas, and fish and chips, and there were sand-hills and sailors, and a park, and a dame school, and a narrow lane at the back, where we also all tried to fly, though we used mackintoshes as cloaks, like Superman. I lived there till I was ten, and then the family moved to Liverpool, and I became 'taffy' for the whole of secondary school, and beyond, though my Welsh accent didn't survive the first form. And yet I never lost the ability to use the accent at will. Regular holidays back to Holyhead kept it alive, and I became quite adept at switching linguistic identities, as occasion demanded. At 5 o'clock on Lime Street Station I would speak a pure scouse that could cut like a knife; by 9 o'clock, leaving Holyhead Station, having successfully negotiated the checkpoint of Llanfair P.G.'s 18 syllables, I was linguistically reborn. I think I remember thinking, how important it was to be seen to belong, to identify with the place and the people, by using their language. So I would give my accent its yearly service, and run it in gently by exchanging Welsh hellos with every old lady polishing her doorstep in Thomas Street.

I cannot remember when I first read Dylan Thomas, or this piece, I seem to have always known it, especially its final line. I remember searching for his books in school, and doing an amalgam of Emlyn Williams and Dylan at innumerable Liverpool parish social evenings, where my Welsh reputation gave me an unquestioned authority to perform such things, regardless of ability.

Then later, I used my English language training to take his poems to pieces, as so many linguists have done, and learned how difficult it was to put them back together again. Yet I do find it helpful still to make use of him in lectures, as a source of illustration of linguistic ingenuity and daring, and of semantic compression – for is it not remarkable how he has packed a world of associations into such phrases as 'everlasting park' and 'lane of confidences'? But for me, his individuality in language was always second to his way of communicating the individuality of a person, a place, a time ... of conveying a sense of human uniqueness, while prompting a sense of universal recognition. What happened in Swansea in the 1920s happened also in Holyhead in the 1940s, and yet it wasn't the same.

Each time I read this story, and its fellows, I find myself host to a flood of recollections, merging childhood and after, Wales and elsewhere, blurring fact and fiction. Why do I remember, now, playing a saxophone in a band, in the first wave of Liverpool pop groups? One evening our group was playing in a hall where the Quarry Men (the embryo Beatles) were later due to play. I remember meeting someone ... I'm fairly sure it was from that group ... in fact, I'm sure it was Paul McCartney ... it definitely could have been ... The story enlarges with time, and for my older children, and those of my students who have heard this rumour, I was almost a Beatle, and my subsequent career has been a long, slow slide downhill. I often wonder, what happened, really? Heaven help anyone who tries to produce coherence in that genre of fiction generally known as autobiography! The memories of adult life have no order and no end, either.

CONSTANCE CUMMINGS
ACTRESS

You've seen a strawberry
   that's had a struggle; yet
   was, where the fragments met,

a hedgehog or a star –
   fish for the multitude
   of seeds. What better food

than apple-seeds – the fruit
   within the fruit – locked in
   like counter-curved twin

hazel-nuts? Frost that kills
   the little rubber-plant –
   leaves of kok-saghyz-stalks, can't

harm the roots; they still grow
   in frozen ground. Once where
   there was a prickly-pear –

leaf clinging to barbed wire,
   a root shot down to grow
   in earth two feet below;

as carrots form mandrakes
   or a ram's-horn root sometimes. Victory won't come

to me unless I go
   to it; a grape-tendril
   ties a knot in knots till

knotted thirty times, – so
   the bound twig that's under –
   gone and over-gone, can't stir.

The weak overcomes its
  menace, the strong overcomes itself. What is there

like fortitude! What sap
  went through that little thread
  to make the cherry red!

'Nevertheless', by Marianne Moore

Marianne Moore is a favourite poet of mine. I love her direct, clear speech.

Her sensitive closeness to all the aspects of nature shows a deep understanding and acceptance which I find extraordinarily and beautifully optimistic.

SIR ROBIN DAY

T.V. AND RADIO JOURNALIST

This royal throne of kings, this scepter'd isle,
This earth of majesty, this seat of Mars,
This other Eden, demi-paradise,
This fortress built by Nature for herself
Against infection and the hand of war,
This happy breed of men, this little world,
This precious stone set in the silver sea,
Which serves it in the office of a wall,
Or as a moat defensive to a house,
Against the envy of less happier lands,
This blessed plot, this earth, this realm, this England ...
This land of such dear souls, this dear, dear land.

From: *The Tragedy of King Richard II*: II: 1, by William
                    Shakespeare

Call them hackneyed, or call them immortal, those lines have passed
into the language. It is unnecessary to explain why I chose them,
except to say they never fail to move me and to hearten me if
I am depressed about my country.

RT HON. LORD DENNING
MASTER OF THE ROLLS

Reviewing the position generally, the chief point which emerges is that we have not yet settled the principles upon which to control the new powers of the executive. No one can suppose that the executive will never be guilty of the sins that are common to all of us. You may be sure that they will sometimes do things which they ought not to do: and will not do things that they ought to do. But if and when wrongs are thereby suffered by any of us, what is the remedy? Our procedure for securing our personal freedom is efficient, but our procedure for preventing the abuse of power is not. Just as the pick and shovel is no longer suitable for the winning of coal, so also the procedure of *mandamus, certiorari*, and actions on the case are not suitable for the winning of freedom in the new age. They must be replaced by new and up to date machinery, by declarations, injunctions, and actions for negligence: and, in judicial matters, by compulsory powers to order a case stated. This is not a task for Parliament. Our representatives there cannot control the day to day activities of the many who administer the manifold activities of the State: nor can they award damages to those who are injured by any abuses. The courts must do this. Of all the great tasks that lie ahead, this is the greatest. Properly exercised the new powers of the executive lead to the welfare state: but abused they lead to the totalitarian state. None such must ever be allowed in this country. We have in our time to deal with changes which are of equal constitutional significance to those which took place 300 years ago. Let us prove ourselves equal to the challenge.

From: *Freedom under the Law*, by Lord Denning

I wrote that in 1949. Now here in 1982 I think we can say that during this intervening time we have improved our procedure greatly for preventing the abuse of power. We have got new and up to date machinery by which judges can review the decisions of tribunals and administrative authorities. The new procedure is called 'judicial reivew'. We have also improved beyond measure the ability of the courts to correct abuses of power in some quarters, but nevertheless there are still very important bodies in the land which the law has been unable to control. We have yet to see whether Parliament will do anything about it.

JONATHAN DIMBLEBY
JOURNALIST AND BROADCASTER

Grey day for the Show, but cars jam the narrow lanes.
Inside, on the field, judging has started: dogs
(Set their legs back, hold out their tails) and ponies (manes
Repeatedly smoothed, to calm heads); over there, sheep
(Cheviot and Blackface); by the hedge, squealing logs
(Chain Saw Competition). Each has its own keen crowd.
In the main arena, more judges meet by a jeep:
The jumping's on next. Announcements, splutteringly loud,

Clash with the quack of a man with pound notes round his hat
And a lit-up board. There's more than just animals:
Bead-stalls, balloon-men, a Bank; a beer-marquee that
Half-screens a canvas Gents; a tent selling tweed,
And another, jackets. Folks sit about on bales
Like great straw dice. For each scene is linked by spaces
Not given to anything much, where kids scrap, freed,
While their owners stare different ways with incurious faces.

The wrestling starts, late; a wide ring of people; then cars;
Then trees; then pale sky. Two young men in acrobats' tights
And embroidered trunks hug each other; rock over the grass,
Stiff-legged, in a two-man scrum. One falls: they shake
                                                    hands.
Two more start, one grey-haired: he wins, though. They're
                                          not so much fights
As long immobile strainings that end in unbalance
With one on his back, unharmed, while the other stands
Smoothing his hair. But there are other talents –

The long high tent of growing and making, wired-off
Wood tables past which crowds shuffle, eyeing the scrubbed
                                                      spaced
Extrusions of earth: blanch leeks like church candles, six
                                                    pods of
Broad beans (one split open), dark shining-leafed cabbages –
                                                        rows
Of single supreme versions, followed (on laced

Paper mats) by dairy and kitchen; four brown eggs, four
                                          white eggs,
Four plain scones, four dropped scones, pure excellences
                                          that enclose
A recession of skills. And, after them, lambing-sticks, rugs,
Needlework, knitted caps, baskets, all worthy, all well done,
But less than the honeycombs. Outside, the jumping's over.
The young ones thunder their ponies in competition
Twice round the ring; then trick races, Musical Stalls,
Sliding off, riding bareback, the ponies dragged to and fro for
Bewildering requirements, not minding. But now, in the
                                          background,
Like shifting scenery, horse-boxes move; each crawls
Towards the stock entrance, tilting and swaying, bound
For far-off farms. The pound-note man decamps.
The car park has thinned. They're loading jumps on a truck.
Back now to private addresses, gates and lamps
In high stone one-street villages, empty at dusk,
And side roads of small towns (sports finals stuck
In front doors, allotments reaching down to the railway);
Back now to autumn, leaving the ended husk
Of summer that brought them here for Show Saturday –

The men with hunters, dog-breeding wool-defined women,
Children all saddle-swank, mugfaced middleaged wives
Glaring at jellies, husbands on leave from the garden
Watchful as weasels, car-tuning curt-haired sons –
Back now, all of them, to their local lives:
To names on vans, and business calendars
Hung up in kitchens; back to loud occasions
In the Corn Exchange, to market days in bars,
To winter coming, as the dismantled Show
Itself dies back into the area of work.
Let it stay hidden there like strength, below
Sale-bills and swindling; something people do,
Not noticing how time's rolling smithy-smoke
Shadows much greater gestures; something they share
That breaks ancestrally each year into
Regenerate union. Let it always be there.

'Show Saturday', by Philip Larkin

66

In the rush of these days I only see those country shows from the upholstered inside of a speeding train: a vague blur of four-legged action over multi-coloured fences, encircled by a doting camp of landrovers and family picnics.

The effect of such a momentary vision is always the same and invariably unsatisfactory. I experience a rush of emotion that is a mixture of delight and anguish for what is irretrievably lost – what we call, dismissively, nostalgia. For once, when summers stood still one after another, and before the sense of mortality began to usurp the joy of the moment, I was one of those children 'all saddle-swank'. I was (to tell the truth) good at it too. I collected cups and rosettes to display at home, which not only exceeded in number the array of tele-prizes awarded to my father, but also exacted a greater admiration from the rest of the family.

When I read 'Show Saturday' I sense again the images, sounds and smells (most of all the smells, and particularly crushed grass and saddle soap) so powerfully, that were it not for Larkin the sense of loss for all that of which the Show was only a small part, would be overwhelming.

But the poet is not merely true to my remembered past, nor is 'Show Saturday' only an affectionate catalogue of a precisely observed and essentially harmless rural tradition. Larkin shapes the images, orders the memory, and most of all, validates and then drives out nostalgia. By refusing to mock, but instead rejoicing in the ordinariness of 'something people do', he reveals that confined within the slightly bumbling and not overly-imaginative custom of the country Show there is a transcendent innocence. And, in an affirmation of human existence that the cold-war warriors should not be allowed to ignore, he urges 'Let it always be there'.

MARGARET DRABBLE

WRITER

Lovely Miss Lindley, striding across the asphalt playground
in her long boots and her short skirt, her long hair bouncing
with the energy of her stride, her face expressing authority,
amusement, conviction, tireless, vain, adored by her infants
basking radiantly in the warmth of their adoration and her
own virtue, reaping each day what she sowed, a whole harvest
of smiles and confidences and hands tugging at her rather
high hem, and voices saying Miss, Miss (or Mum when they
forgot it was Miss). Guess what, Miss, you'll never guess.
It was a job she was doing, and she loved it. Lovely Miss
Lindley, striding across the asphalt playground to that
building that looked like a prison but thanks to her and people
like her was not one: let her so forever stride, ask no questions
about her future or her past, her motives, her endurance,
do not ask when that youthful energy will fail her, but let
her walk across that playground in her sexy boots, perfect,
accomplished, across and across, again and again, her hair
bouncing, a cheerful commitment and dedication in her very
step. Do not seek to disbelieve it, do not disturb her with
disbelief, because she is, there she walks, towards that ever-
waiting classroom, and as she opens the door she will smile,
greeting their smiles, she will receive with love that daunting
chorus of demands, claims, cries and exhortations. Do not
believe that she does not, could not exist. O lovely Miss
Lindley. O almost confident apostrophe.

From: *The Needle's Eye*, by Margaret Drabble

I had originally thought I might be able to find a passage about
speech difficulties, as I suffered myself very severely as a child
from a stammer, which still intermittently silences me, or forces
me to ask for a ticket to Green Park instead of Leicester Square
– but I find that I've never written about the problem. Perhaps
it is too close. Certainly I know that I am very sensitive about
comic portrayals of any form of speech problem. Maybe I will write
about it one day.

I chose the passage about Miss Lindley for several reasons. One is nostalgia – she is a primary school teacher, an amalgam of various real teachers who taught my children when they were small, at a school near the Arsenal football stadium, then at another at New End in Hampstead. Both were grim buildings with concrete playgrounds, and both had marvellous staff. So whenever I remember this passage, I also think of those tense, tired, wonderfully touching years of collecting small children from school, which seemed at the time interminable, but now seem such a brief period of life, and in retrospect so enjoyable – the camaraderie of mums in the playground, the extraordinary social mix of children in a London school, the jokes and the gossip and the excitement of new maths and prisms and keeping guinea pigs and school journeys comes back to me very strongly with Miss Lindley. I also like it because it places the mini-skirt. By the end of this novel Miss Lindley has gone into maxi-skirts. She was a fashion-conscious young woman. It was while noting such things that I began to aspire to keep the record, as a novelist, to catch change even as it happens. And lastly, I like Miss Lindley because she was an idealist, and a hard working one. Teachers don't realise how lastingly their pupils remember them, and how profoundly influential are all their little kindnesses. This was an attempt to thank them.

PAUL EDDINGTON

ACTOR

As you set out for Ithaka
hope your road is a long one,
full of adventure, full of discovery.
Laistrygonians, Cyclops,
angry Poseidon – don't be afraid of them:
you'll never find things like that on your way
as long as you keep your thoughts raised high,
as long as a rare excitement
stirs your spirit and your body.
Laistrygonians, Cyclops,
wild Poseidon – you won't encounter them
unless you bring them along inside your soul,
unless your soul sets them up in front of you.

Hope your road is a long one.
May there be many summer mornings when,
with what pleasure, what joy,
you enter harbours you're seeing for the first time;
may you stop at Phoenician trading stations
to buy fine things,
mother of pearl and coral, amber and ebony,
sensual perfume of every kind –
as many sensual perfumes as you can;
and may you visit many Egyptian cities
to learn and go on learning from their scholars.

Keep Ithaka always in your mind.
Arriving there is what you're destined for.
But don't hurry the journey at all.
Better if it lasts for years,
so you're old by the time you reach the island,
wealthy with all you've gained on the way,
not expecting Ithaka to make you rich.

Ithaka gave you the marvellous journey.
Without her you wouldn't have set out.
She has nothing left to give you now.

And if you find her poor, Ithaka won't have fooled you.
Wise as you will have become, so full of experience,
you'll have understood by then what these Ithakas mean.

'Ithaka', by C. P. Cavafy (translated by Edmund Keeley
and Philip Sherrard)

I chose this poem because it advocates a calm acceptance of life
with its pleasures and vicissitudes which I wish I myself could
emulate – but I don't suppose I ever shall.

He had been round the office canvassing opinions about the subjects of conversation proper to countrymen. 'Mangel-wurzels are a safe topic,' he had been told, 'only you mustn't call them that. It's a subject on which farmers are very touchy. Call them roots ...'

He greeted William with cordiality. 'Ah, Boot, how are you? Don't think I've had the pleasure before. Know your work well of course. Sit down. Have a cigarette or' – had he made a floater? – 'or do you prefer your churchwarden?'

William took a cigarette. He and Mr Salter sat opposite one another. Between them, on the desk, lay an open atlas in which Mr Salter had been vainly trying to find Reykjavik.

There was a pause, during which Mr Salter planned a frank and disarming opening. 'How are your roots, Boot?' It came out wrong.

'How are your boots, root?' he asked.

William, glumly awaiting some fulminating rebuke, started and said, 'I beg your pardon?'

'I mean brute,' said Mr Salter.

William gave it up. Mr Salter gave it up. They sat staring at one another, fascinated, hopeless. Then:

'How's hunting?' asked Mr Salter, trying a new line. 'Foxes pretty plentiful?'

'Well, we stop in the summer, you know.'

'Do you? Everyone away, I suppose?'

Another pause: 'Lot of foot and mouth, I expect,' said Mr Salter hopefully.

'None, I'm thankful to say.'

'Oh!'

Their eyes fell. They both looked at the atlas before them.

'You don't happen to know where Reykjavik is?'

'No.'

'Pity. I hoped you might. No one in the office does.'

'Was that what you wanted to see me about?'

'Oh, no, not at all! Quite the contrary.'

Another pause.

William saw what was up. This decent little man had been

deputed to sack him and could not get it out. He came to the rescue. 'I expect you want to talk about the great crested grebe.'

'Good God, no,' said Mr Salter, with instinctive horror, adding politely, 'At least not unless *you* do.'

'No, not at all,' said William, 'I thought *you* might want to.'

'Not at all,' said Mr Salter.

'That's all right, then.'

'Yes, that all right . . .' Desperately: 'I say, how about some zider?'

'Zider?'

'Yes. I expect you feel like a drop of zider about this time, don't you? We'll go out and have some.'

The journalists in the film had been addicted to straight rye. Silent but wondering, William followed the foreign editor. They shared the lift with a very extraordinary man, bald, young, fleshless as a mummy, dressed in brown and white checks, smoking a cheroot. 'He does the Sports Page now,' said Mr Salter apologetically, when he was out of hearing.

In the public house at the corner, where *The Beast* reporters congregated, the barmaid took their order with surprise. 'Cider? I'll see.' Then she produced two bottles of sweet and fizzy liquid. William and Mr Salter sipped suspiciously.

'Not quite what you're used to down on the farm, I'm afraid.'

'Well, to tell you the truth, I don't often drink it. We give it to the haymakers, of course, and I sometimes have some of theirs.' Then, fearing that this might sound snobbish, he added, 'My Uncle Bernard drinks it for his rheumatism.'

'You're sure you wouldn't sooner have something else?'

'No.'

'You mean you wouldn't?'

'I mean I would.'

'Really?'

'Really; much sooner.'

'Good for you, Garge,' said Mr Salter, and from that moment a new, more human note was apparent in their relationship; conversation was still far from easy, but they had this bond in common, that neither of them liked cider.

From: *Scoop*, by Evelyn Waugh

Scoop is a satirical novel about Fleet Street where the Daily Beast and Daily Brute slog it out. Lord Copper, the megalomaniac owner of the Beast wants to send Boot the novelist to a war in Africa. He so instructs his Foreign Editor Mr Salter. Mr Salter makes a mistake and the man who answers his summons is Mr William Boot who writes the country notes 'Lush Places' for the paper. He thinks he is being summoned to the office for a rebuke over an error. The Foreign Editor knows nothing about the country and prepares anxiously for the interview to despatch Mr Boot to Africa. The extract shows what ensues.

It has always struck me as a marvellous piece of comic writing. It is economical. The scene is set very well. It is particularly interesting for students of prose to note the shortness of the sentences and the vigour and rhythm of the construction.

SIR ROGER FALK O.B.E.
CHAIRMAN OF ACTION FOR DYSPHASIC ADULTS

The specialty of rule hath been neglected:
And look, how many Grecian tents do stand
Hollow upon this plain, so many hollow factions.
When that the general is not like the hive
To whom the foragers shall all repair,
What honey is expected? Degree being vizarded,
The unworthiest shows as fairly in the mask.
The heavens themselves, the planets, and this centre
Observe degree, priority, and place,
Insisture, course, proportion, season, form,
Office, and custom, in all line of order:
And therefore is the glorious planet Sol
In noble eminence enthron'd and spher'd
Amidst the other; whose med'cinable eye
Corrects the ill aspects of planets evil,
And posts, like the commandment of a king,
Sans check, to good and bad: but when the planets
In evil mixture to disorder wander,
What plagues, and what portents, what mutiny,
What raging of the sea, shaking of earth,
Commotion in the winds, frights, changes, horrors,
Divert and crack, rend and deracinate
The unity and married calm of states
Quite from their fixure! O! when degree is shak'd,
Which is the ladder to all high designs,
The enterprise is sick. How could communities,
Degrees in schools, and brotherhoods in cities,
Peaceful commerce from dividable shores,
The primogenitive and due of birth,
Prerogative of age, crowns, sceptres, laurels,
But by degree, stand in authentic place?
Take but degree away, untune that string,
And, hark! what discord follows; each thing meets
In mere oppugnancy: the bounded waters
Should lift their bosoms higher than the shores,
And make a sop of all this solid globe:
Strength should be lord of imbecility,

And the rude son should strike his father dead
Force should be right; or rather, right and wrong –
Between whose endless jar justice resides –
Should lose their names, and so should justice too.
Then every thing includes itself in power,
Power into will, will into appetite;
And appetite, a universal wolf,
So doubly seconded with will and power,
Must make perforce a universal prey,
And last eat up himself. Great Agamemnon,
This chaos, when degree is suffocate,
Follows the choking.
And this neglection of degree it is
That by a pace goes backward, with a purpose
It hath to climb. The general's disdain'd
By him one step below, he by the next,
That next by him beneath; so every step,
Exampled by the first pace that is sick
Of his superior, grows to an envious fever
Of pale and bloodless emulation:
And 'tis this fever that keeps Troy on foot,
Not her own sinews. To end a tale of length
Troy in our weakness lives, not in her strength.

From: *Troilus and Cressida*: I: 3, by William Shakespeare

I have chosen the lines from Ulysses' marvellous speech to the
assembled Greek Generals outside the gates of Troy (which they
are unable to subdue) as my contribution to the anthology. To
me this speech and the ideas it conveys is Shakespeare at his wisest,
most perceptive and, in today's grievous situation all over the
world, most relevant. In many speeches I have had to give where
I am trying to make my audience think in constructive terms I
have quoted bits – and occasionally all of it – because, to me, despite
the fact that the play itself of *Troilus and Cressida* is not one of
Shakespeare's best (and I am no authority; merely an ardent lover
of Shakespeare) Ulysses' speech, so early in the play, justifies all
the rest!

BERT FOORD
METEOROLOGIST

If you can keep you head when all about you
Are losing theirs and blaming it on you,
If you can trust yourself when all men doubt you,
But make allowance for their doubting too;
If you can wait and not be tired by waiting,
Or being lied about, don't deal in lies,
Or being hated, don't give way to hating,
And yet don't look too good, nor talk too wise:

If you can dream, – and not make dreams your master
If you can think – and not make thoughts your aim
If you can meet with Triumph and Disaster
And treat these two imposters just the same;
If you can bear to hear the truth you've spoken
Twisted by knaves to make a trap for fools,
Or watch the things you gave your life to, broken,
And stoop and build 'em up with worn-out tools;

If you can make one heap of all your winnings
And risk it on one turn of pitch-and-toss,
And lose, and start again at your beginnings
And never breathe a word about your loss;
If you can force your heart and nerve and sinew
To serve your turn long after they are gone,
And so hold on when there is nothing in you
Except the Will which says to them: 'Hold on!'

If you can walk with crowds and keep your virtue
Or walk with kings – nor lose the common touch,
If neither foes nor loving friends can hurt you
If all men count with you, but not too much;
If you can fill the unforgiving minute
With sixty seconds' worth of distance run,
Yours is the Earth and everything that's in it,
And – which is more – you'll be a Man, my son!

'If', by Rudyard Kipling

Of all the poems I have read – and I prefer the epic style rather than the romantic – this one contains most of the virtues and upholds all the old standards which unfortunately seem to be collapsing in our present day lives. It preaches humility, honesty, steadfastness under adversity, a cool head in a crisis, hard work and many other pillars of the old moral code which we British stood for in days gone by. However, recent speeches by politicians during the Falklands Crisis seem to have stressed the old virtues, so perhaps the old moral values are just under the surface and have been suppressed rather than discarded altogether. Any young person who strives to follow the advice in the poem would be a very pleasant person to deal with and would find day-to-day life much happier and easier to bear, even if times are hard.

JOHN FOWLES
WRITER

There is a day a dreadfull day
Still following the past
When sun and moon are past away
And mingle with the blast
There is a vision in my eye
A vacuum oer my mind
Sometimes as on the sea I lye
Mid roaring waves and wind

When valleys rise to mountain waves
And mountains sink to seas
When towns and cities temples graves
All vanish like a breeze
The skyes that was are past and oer
That almanack of days
Year chronicles are kept no more
Oblivions ruin pays

Pays in destruction shades and hell
Sin goes in darkness down
And therein sulphurs shadows dwell
Worth wins and wears the crown
The very shore if shore I see
All shrivelled to a scroll
The Heaven's rend away from me
And thunders sulphurs roll

Black as the deadly thunder cloud
The stars shall turn to dun
And heaven by that darkness bowed
Shall make days light be done
When stars and skys shall all decay
And earth no more shall be
When heaven itself shall pass away
Then thou'lt remember me

'Song Last Day', by John Clare

John Clare is my favourite English poet. The world at large still seems to view him as his own time did, as little more than a curiosity, an odd man out in the complacent stream of 'educated' English poetry. A tinge of that patronizing label he was first given, 'the Northamptonshire Peasant', still clings to his name. Clare *was* a peasant; but also, a peasant genius. I love three things about him. The first is his astounding simplicity and accuracy of description, a faculty in which he leaves every other English nature-poet a hundred fields behind; the second, his ever-green compassion for humbler forms of life; and the third, his lack of education, both general and poetic. This last once elicited one of the crassest remarks ('I have often remarked that your poetry is much the best when you are not describing common things') ever made by a London publisher to an author. It is true that Clare could be very uncouth and wild, technically, in some of his verse; but even that 'clumsiness' is really a function of a far nobler kind of wildness, a mark of how far apart he stands from the way most middle-class writers approach nature. They always try to tidy it, to garden with their words. Clare's all-seeing eyes set it direct, without artifice.

The poem I have chosen shows this wildness, both of technique and deeper vision. It survives only in a scribbled draft written some time in the 1840s, after madness had already struck him down, and I can never read it without thinking of nuclear holocaust. It is rough, repetitive, stuttering to the point of incoherence. Yet it has always seemed to me one of the strangest fragments of verse in our language, rivalled in underlying force only by that other great poet-seer, William Blake. For all his other misfortunes, Clare never suffered from dysphasia; yet something in 'There is a day a dreadful day' will, I hope, speak especially to those who do have to live with a vision in the eye and a vacuum in the mind.

ROY FULLER
POET

Sweet semi-circled Cynthia played at maw,
The whilst Endymion ran the wild-goose chase:
Great Bacchus with his cross-bow killed a daw,
And sullen Saturn smiled with pleasant face:
The ninefold Bugbears of the Caspian lake
Sat whistling ebon hornpipes to their ducks;
Madge-owlet straight for joy her girdle brake,
And rugged Satyrs frisked like stags and bucks:
The untamed tumbling fifteen-footed Goat
With promulgation of the Lesbian shores
Confronted Hydra in a sculler boat,
At which the mighty mountain Taurus roars:
    Meantime great Sultan Soliman was born,
    And Atlas blew his rustic rumbling horn.

'Mockado, Fustian, and Motley', by John Taylor

When I first read Norman Ault's still fascinating *A Treasury of Unfamilar Lyrics* (1938), I was struck by one poem especially, a sonnet by John Taylor. Taylor lived from 1580 and 1653, called himself 'The Water Poet', had been in the Navy, was a Thames bargee – a comic writer of many facets who in our time might have contributed to *Beyond the Fringe* or *Monty Python's Flying Circus*. The sonnet in question is nonsense, though each of its notions has a kind of wild logic. Thus, to take the first line, Cynthia = Diana = the moon = Queen Elizabeth (?); and she is 'semi-circled' because of the bows both of the goddess and of the moon. Is it because she was also worshipped under the name Trivia that she 'played at maw' (a card game using the piquet pack)? Who knows what other meanings may have been there for the poem's contemporary readers?

The poem's references are fun to track down (with, say, Lemprière and Brewer and the OED), but surely it makes a great effect on a simple reading. No doubt its object is to send up the classical references, and latinate and generally highfalutin language so fashionable and carried seriously to such lengths in Taylor's period. But in doing so it creates its own poetic magic: 'The ninefold Bugbears of the Caspian lake' – what a marvellous line! Do we care whether or not there is an explanation of it? It reverberates like the often imperfectly understood (or ununderstandable!) lines of some modern poets, like Dylan Thomas and Wallace Stevens – only just on the wrong side of what I myself would consider fair play in poetry, an art which indubitably relies to a fair extent on verbal riddling and sonority, to say nothing of more or less erudite reference.

INDIRA GANDHI
PRIME MINISTER OF INDIA

Where the mind is without fear and
the head is held high;
Where knowledge is free;
Where the world has not been broken
up into fragments by narrow domestic
walls;
Where words come out from the
depth of truth;
Where tireless striving stretches its
arms towards perfection;
Where the clear stream of reason has
not lost its way into the dreary desert
sand of dead habit;
Where the mind is led forward by
thee into ever-widening thought and
action –
Into that heaven of freedom, my
Father, let my country awake.

From: *Gitanjali* (Song Offerings) by Rabindra Nath Tagore

This is one of my favourite poems. It is a prayer by our great
Nobel Laureate, Rabindra Nath Tagore. I wish I could make it
our national anthem.

JOHN GANT
DOCTOR

As I was climbing Ardan Mór
From the shore of Sheelin lake,
I met the herons coming down
Before the waters wake.

And they were talking in their flight
Of dreamy ways the herons go
When all the hills are withered up
Nor any waters flow.

'Ardan Mór', by Francis Ledwidge

Francis Ledwidge was killed in the first World War. It was in 1917. He was 26.

To give reasons for the choice is difficult. I'm no literary critic or analyst – only someone who enjoyed words, and envied those who were able to weave them – more so since, for all practical purposes, I've grown mute.

With hindsight, I must – like many people – have been a slipshod talker. Only when words fail to slip off the tongue is their absolute value appreciated too late. We take our functions too much for granted.

Now words buzz round my brain like bottled bees – and by the time my larynx has been redded up to utter them, their relevance has passed. It's extremely galling.

There's no penetrating and perspicacious slice of considered reasoning to go with the poem. I could have used recondite words – like The Critics – which I always have to look up. The best I can say is that most good verse seldom declares its content openly – it gives suggestions, half-formed, for the imagination to play with. Like music, it should hold elusive images.

BAMBER GASCOIGNE
WRITER and BROADCASTER

Lovers in the act dispense
With such meum-tuum sense
As might warningly reveal
What they must not pick or steal,
And their nostrum is to say:
'I and you are both away'.

After when they disentwine
You from me and yours from mine,
Neither can be certain who
Was that I whose mine was you.
To the act again they go
More completely not to know.

Theft is theft and raid is raid
Though reciprocally made.
Lovers, the conclusion is
Doubled sighs and jealousies
In a single heart that grieves
For lost honour among thieves.

'The Thieves', by Robert Graves

A favourite poem since schooldays. It combines superbly the
intellectual and the sexy, two fields in which my friends and I
were eager to excel. My classical studies (compulsory and disliked)
had at least equipped me to enjoy the pun in 'nostrum', and I
marvelled then, and marvel still, at the verbal ingenuity and
economy of 'Neither can be certain who/Was that I whose mine
was you'. In the Penguin anthology entitled *Contemporary Verse*,
edited by Kenneth Allott, the first two verses were on one page
and you had to turn over to reach the third verse. I was an addict
of the poem before I discovered there was a third verse, and I
still find the worldly-wise pessimism of the single grieving heart
less seductive than the playful romanticism of the opening. I very
much preferred the idea of to the act again going and more
completely not knowing – or, in terms of reading the poem, being

directed back to the beginning of verse 1 from the end of verse 2. If in your anthology you manage to print it with verse 2 at the bottom of a recto page, as Mr Allott did, then your readers, too, will have the fortunate option provided to me as a schoolboy.

[Editor's note: we didn't, but hope that the poem is still enjoyable!]

GERMAINE GREER
WRITER

When all the over-work of life
   Is finished once, and fast asleep
We swerve no more beneath the knife
   But taste that silence cool and deep;
Forgetful of the highways rough,
   Forgetful of the thorny scourge,
   Forgetful of the tossing surge,
Then shall we find it is enough?

How can we say 'enough' on earth –
   'Enough' with such a craving heart?
I have not found it since my birth,
   But still have bartered part for part.
I have not held and hugged the whole,
   But paid the old to gain the new:
   Much have I paid, yet much is due,
Till I am beggared sense and soul.

I used to labour, used to strive
   For pleasure with a restless will:
Now if I save my soul alive
   All else what matters good or ill?
I used to dream alone, to plan
   Unspoken hopes and days to come:–
   Of all my past this is the sum –
I will not lean on child of man.

To give, to give, not to receive!
   I long to pour myself, my soul,
Not to keep back or count or leave,
   But king with king to give the whole.
I long for one to stir my deep –
   I have had enough of help and gift –
   I long for one to search and sift
Myself, to take myself and keep.

You scratch my surface with your pin,
   You stroke me smooth with hushing breath:–

Nay pierce, nay probe, nay dig within,
 Probe my quick core and sound my depth.
You call me with a puny call,
 You talk, you smile, you nothing do:
 How should I spend my heart on you,
My heart that so outweighs you all?

Your vessels are by much too strait:
 Were I to pour, you could not hold. –
 Bear with me: I must bear to wait,
 A fountain sealed through heat and cold.
Bear with me days or months or years:
 Deep must call deep until the end
 When friend shall no more envy friend
Nor vex his friend at unawares.

Not in this world of hope deferred,
 This world of perishable stuff:–
Eye hath not seen nor ear hath heard
 Nor heart conceived that full 'enough':
Here moans the separating sea,
 Here harvests fail, here breaks the heart:
 There God shall join and no man part,
I full of Christ and Christ of me.

'The Heart Knoweth its own Bitterness', by Christina
Rossetti

Christina Rossetti is the great poet of the unlived life and the
unspoken word. She was only twenty-six when she wrote this
poem, which bears ample signs of her usual hasty composition
and unwillingness to revise, yet its jagged and slightly contradictory
course follows the contour of a powerful and passionate mind which
is totally frustrated. Rossetti would never have uttered these words
aloud; the frightening middle stanzas of the poem with their
dreadful contempt and bitterness, are written, as it were, behind
clenched teeth. Her biographers would have earned her scorn, for
they are all fascinated by the question of the identity of the man
who broke her heart. In this poem, for those who have wit to
understand it, she describes disappointment with love itself, in
terms of the human incapacity for communion. All the energy of
the poem is generated in the statement of disgust; the vision of

the communion of saints is perfunctory by comparison, as well as mildly heretical. She is now remembered as the poet of graceful Victorian piety: actually her life was a long agony of self-repression, eventually, inevitably, complicated by ill-health. It may well be that her very occasional outbursts of fury and despair will come to mean more to us than the poetry she stilled her pounding heart to write.

As you see, the poem does not celebrate the power of words but rather the impotence of words; nevertheless the imagery of the sealed fountain is immediately relevant, and it sometimes helps to have someone else's powerful words to utter instead of groaning.

LEON GRIFFITHS
WRITER

In the spring of 1954 Whitey Bimstein and Freddie Brown
told me about a new talent confided to their care who was
outré but interesting. 'A nanimal', Mr Bimstein said. 'A
throwback to the man of the gutter.' 'A mental case,' Mr
Brown agreed, without disapproval in his voice. 'By that I
mean he's got to be doing something all the time.' Managers,
like book publishers, make most of the money, but trainers,
like editors, participate more directly in the artists' labours.
Bimstein and Brown are editors of prizefighters. Mediocrity
depresses them; they are excited by talent, even latent. What
they dream about is genius, but unfortunately that is harder
to identify.

Technically, Whitey and Freddie can do a lot for a fighter
– excise redundant gesture and impose a severe logic of
punching, as demonstrable as old-fashioned mathematics ...
It is the psyche that makes Freddie and Whitey sweat. Like
authors, fighters of exemplary moral quality may be bores.
And fighters who do a lot of beautiful things nobody else
does may be children emotionally. The good boys get
married. The bad ones get in jams. It is hard to tell which
may mean more trouble for trainers. 'The worst trouble
is assorted maniacs,' Whitey says, 'because you never know
when it is going to break out.'...

I have known Whitey for more than twenty years (he has
been a trainer for fifteen years before that), and by now I
can tell from looking at him whether he thinks genius is
lurking just the other side of the horizon. Four years ago
he was desperate for talent. Prosperity had ruined the future,
he said; any kid just out of school could get a job for sixty
dollars a week, and as a consequence dillettantism was rife
in boxing. The faintest frown of fortune would send a boy
back to well-paid labour. Boys boxed only to attain social
prestige. 'Garbage,' Whitey said then, when I asked him
about the season's vintage. But this spring he was wearing
the expression of an editor who has found two new poets
and a woman novelist with an acid talent. The mild recession
was not solely responsible, he said, although it had made

the boys more serious about it as a vocation. He and Freddie had three good fighters at once – two lightweights and one around '30 (130 pounds) who could do '26 to qualify as featherweight. They also had this animal, Whitey said, who ran fifteen or twenty miles a day on the road and would box fifteen rounds every day if they would let him. Whitey was in the position of the late Max Perkins, with a handful of good established writers and a Thomas Wolfe in training in Brooklyn.

I asked him how big the animal was, and he said it was a coloured heavyweight, six feet one and a half and over '90. 'His name is Tommy Jackson,' he said. 'Until you know, you don't know what you got to put up with.'

(*Note: Liebling was not impressed by Jackson. He won his fights by inducing exhaustion in his opponents. Whitey says 'He is an instinctive fighter'. But Liebling wondered why his friends were taking Jackson seriously, considering his weird life-style like shooting mice, only eating hot-dogs and drinking five bottles of Coca Cola before a fight. – L.G.*)

On the night of the fight, I was more excited than I had been before a match for years, and for subjective reasons. If the animal won, it meant that the Sweet Science was mere guesswork, requiring not even a specialised intelligence. It would be quite a different thing from the victories of immortals like Griffo and Dutch Sam, who were irresponsibles only when they were *outside* the ring. There have been plenty of musicians and painters who didn't have much sense otherwise, and Dostoevski was a political imbecile. I had nothing against Jackson *qua* Jackson, and I wished Whitey and Freddie all kinds of luck with their more conventional clients, but if the animal could beat even a fair fighter, it meant that two hundred and fifty years of painfully acquired experience had been lost to the human race; science was a washout and art a vanity, and Freddie and Whitey had queered their own game.

(*Note: In the event Jackson was beaten by Nino Valdes in the second round by a technical knockout.*)

'Nino and a Nanimal', from *The Sweet Science*, by A. J. Liebling

That fine American essayist A. J. Liebling, who surpassed mere journalism, had a quirky view of the demi-monde and an acute ear for day-to-day speech.

He loved prize-fighting; but even more he loved the prize-fighters and the managers and trainers. Give him a whiff of resin and a smack of leather, a cold beer and an old fighter to reminisce and Liebling could box the ears off Hazlitt.

I missed him when I was recovering from my bout of brain damage. Suddenly, Liebling was too clever by half; the sentences were too tricky and I couldn't understand the metaphors and analogies and I couldn't smile at the jokes. A favourite and familiar friend had become a stranger.

You can't beat pathology, they say. But at least you can try. For myself, I maybe losing on points but it's still going to be a storming finish. Now I can read Liebling. He is my personal yardstick of improvement. I read him slowly, savouring each word (which is probably the best way to read anyway). It's not so much love at first sight, more like a maturing relationship. Good prose suggests clear thought. It's not only good therapy for the mind but also for the soul. Liebling has become a friend again.

Dysphasics come in different sizes and weights and there is no pattern and there are no fringe benefits. I couldn't read Thackeray before and I'm not going to try now. I can't play the piano now. But mind you, I couldn't play before. As Liebling says, with a wry aside, about the trainer of the hapless Tommy Jackson: 'Optimism is the besetting disease of all lovers of the arts'.

SIR ALEC GUINNESS

ACTOR

Mary stood in the kitchen
　　Baking a loaf of bread.
An angel flew in through the window
　　'We've a job for you,' he said.

'God in his big gold heaven,
　　Sitting in his big blue chair,
Wanted a mother for his little son.
　　Suddenly saw you there.'

Mary shook and trembled,
　　'It isn't true what you say.'
'Don't say that,' said the angel.
　　'The baby's on its way.'

Joseph was in the workshop
　　Planing a piece of wood.
'The old man's past it,' the neighbours said.
　　'That girl's been up to no good.'

'And who was that elegant fellow,'
　　They said, 'in the shiny gear?'
The things they said about Gabriel
　　Were hardly fit to hear.

Mary never answered,
　　Mary never replied.
She kept the information,
　　Like the baby, safe inside.

It was election winter.
　　They went to vote in town.
When Mary found her time had come
　　The hotels let her down.

The baby was born in an annexe
　　Next to the local pub.
At midnight, a delegation
　　Turned up from the Farmers' Club.

They talked about an explosion
　　That made a hole in the sky,
Said they'd been sent to the Lamb & Flag
　　To see God come down from on high.

A few days later a bishop
　　And a five-star general were seen
With the head of an African country
　　In a bullet-proof limousine.

'We've come,' they said, 'with tokens
　　For the little boy to choose.'
Told the tale about war and peace
　　In the television news.

After them came the soldiers
　　With rifle and bomb and gun,
Looking for enemies of the state.
　　The family had packed and gone.

He finished up in the papers.
　　He came to a very bad end.
He was charged with bringing the living to life.
　　No man was that prisoner's friend.

There's only one kind of punishment
　　To fit that kind of a crime.
They rigged a trial and shot him dead.
　　They were only just in time.

They lifted the young man by the leg,
　　They lifted him by the arm,
They locked him in a cathedral
　　In case he came to harm.

They stored him safe as water
  Under seven rocks.
One Sunday morning he burst out
  Like a jack-in-the-box.

Through the town he went walking.
  He showed them the holes in his head.
Now do you want any loaves? he cried.
  'Not today,' they said.

When they got back to the village
  The neighbours said, to a man,
'That boy will never be one of us,
  Though he does what he blessed well can.'

He went round to all the people
  A paper crown on his head.
Here is some bread from my father.
  Take, eat, he said.

Nobody seemed very hungry.
  Nobody seemed to care.
Nobody saw the god in himself
  Quietly standing there.

'Ballad of the Bread Man', by Charles Causley

LORD HAILSHAM OF
ST MARYLEBONE

If all the lies I ever told
  Came home to roost with me,
Why, what a merry rookery
  My barren head would be.

For where there's neither leaf nor bud
  But only empty nests,
A thousand inky bills would preen
  A thousand brazen breasts.

And there would be a merry din
  Of beating wings and cries,
For they were mostly merry things,
  My dear departed lies.

How sweet to watch them planing home
  Before the night falls cold,
And see the sunset's fingers turn
  Their sables into gold.

But, ah! It is in vain I build
  A rookery in Spain.
Neither our joys nor yet our sins
  May visit us again.

'Traveller's Song', by The Hon. Neil Hogg

This poem speaks for itself. It illustrates my brother's brilliant versification, and his vein of comic melancholy.

MARGARET HATFIELD

SPEECH-THERAPIST

This darksome burn, horseback brown,
His rollrock highroad roaring down,
In coop and in comb the fleece of his foam
Flutes and low to the lake falls home.

The windpuff-bonnet of fáwn-fróth
Turns and twindles over the broth
Of a pool so pitchblack, féll-frowning,
It rounds and rounds Despair to drowning.

Degged with dew, dappled with dew
Are the groins of the braes that the brook treads through,
Wiry heathpacks, flitches of fern,
And the beadbonny ash that sits over the burn.

What would the world be, once bereft
Of wet and of wildness? Let them be left,
O let them be left, wildness and wet;
Long live the weeds and the wilderness yet.

'Inversnaid', by Gerard Manley Hopkins

I find delight in words and in the rhythms of speech; that is, in part, the reason why the poems of Gerard Manley Hopkins have a special appeal for me. Among a range of subjects, his poetry is concerned with the strong, bright, colourful effects on the senses produced by natural phenomena. In this poem he presents the sight and sound of a wild Scottish burn and pleads passionately for the preservation of 'wildness and wet'. Some sixty years later this plea would have become still more urgent, with what remains of wilderness in our overcrowded island becoming rapidly submerged under the concrete and the tarmac. Gerard Manley Hopkins would see our present existence, bland and aseptic for the fortunate, drab for the less fortunate, and our overdependence on passive substitute experiences through radio and television as the antithesis of all he epitomises in his poem. I share his love of rivers, shores and hillsides, of wildness without violence.

But I also like to be surrounded by words, to have as many books on my shelves as space will allow, to have a few gramophone records of fine actors such as John Gielgud and Laurence Olivier reciting Shakespeare – better still, hear them in the flesh – to live in a sea of endless scraps of paper with handwritten words on them, a by-product of my work. I often have to use words actively: clearly, I have not the mastery of Hopkins, but I can usually cobble together enough words to create a serviceable item. An awareness of the need for words and of their source of delight and solace lies behind what I feel to be my vocation, to try to help others to regain spoken and written language after brain damage. These attempts are seldom completely successful, but there is an aspect of language, the rhythmical, the sonorous and the sensuous, which may sometimes come through more clearly than the intellectual. And that applies to all of us.

BERNARD HEPTON
ACTOR

A moot point
Whether I was going to
Make it.
I just had the strength
To ring the bell.

There were monks inside
And one of them
Eventually
Opened the door.
Oh
He said,
This is a bit of a turn-up
He said
For the book.
Opportune
He said
Your arriving at this particular
As it were
Moment

You're dead right
I said
It was touch and go
Whether I could have managed
To keep going
For very much
Longer.

No
He said
The reason I used the word opportune
Is that
Not to put too fine a point on it
One of our St Bernard dogs is
Unfortunately
Missing.

Oh, dear
I said.
Not looking for me, I hope.

No
He said.
It went for a walk
And got lost in the snow.

Dreadful thing
I said
To happen.

Yes
He said.
It is.

To
Of all creatures
I said
A St Bernard dog
That has devoted
Its entire
Life
To doing good
And helping
Others.

What I was actually thinking
He said
Since you happen to be
In a manner of speaking
Out there already
Is that
If you could
At all
See your way clear
To having a scout
As it were
Around,
It would save one of us

Having to
If I can so put it
Turn out.
Ah
I said
That would
I suppose
Make a kind of sense.

Before you go
He said
If I can find it
You'd better
Here it is
Take this.

What is it?
I said
It's a flask
He said
Of Brandy.
Ah
I said.

For the dog
He said.

Good thinking
I said.

The drill
He said
When you find it
If you ever do
Is to lie down.

Right
I said
Will do.

Lie down on top of it
He said
To keep it warm
Till help arrives.

That was a week ago, and my hopes are rising all the time.
I feel with ever-increasing confidence
that once I can safely say that I am within what might
be called striking distance of knowing where, within a
square mile or two, to start getting down to looking,
my troubles are more or less, to all intents and
purposes, apart from frostbite, with any luck once
help arrives at long last, God willing, as good as over.
It is good to be spurred on with hope.

'One of our St Bernard Dogs is Missing', by N. F. Simpson

This poem is, for me, quite simply, provocative, amusing, witty;
unforgettable. Had I not already been a great admirer of Mr Simpson's very particular writings when I first read it some years ago,
this poem alone would have made me indebted to him.

JAMES HERRIOT
VET AND WRITER

I met a traveller from an antique land
Who said: Two vast and trunkless legs of stone
Stand in the desert ... Near them, on the sand,
Half shrunk, a shattered visage lies, whose frown,
And wrinkled lip, and sneer of cold command,
Tell that its sculptor well those passions read
Which yet survive, stamped on these lifeless things,
The hand that mocked them, and the heart that fed;
And on the pedestal these words appear:
My name is Ozymandias, King of Kings:
Look on my works, ye Mighty, and despair!
Nothing beside remains. Round the decay
Of that colossal wreck, boundless and bare
The lone and level sands stretch far away,

'Ozymandias', by Percy Bysshe Shelley

I first read this poem as a schoolboy and even then its message was vivid and compelling. And, half a century later, it still speaks to me with undimmed certainty.

Of course there is nothing original in pointing out the ephemeral nature of material things and worldly achievements, but Shelley's exquisite use of language adds a deeper meaning to the old truth. A healthy self-esteem is essential for happiness, but it is so easy for people who have tasted the heady wine of success and public acclaim to gain an absurdly inflated impression of their importance in the scheme of things. It is similarly easy for those who have experienced only failure to think that instant happiness is to be found up there in the world of fame.

All these people should read 'Ozymandias'. It is good therapy.

LORD HILL NORTON
ADMIRAL OF THE FLEET

Death is nothing at all. I have only slipped away into the next room. I am I and you are you: Whatever we were to each other, that we are still. Call me by my old familiar name, speak to me in the easy way which you always used. Put no difference into your tone: wear no forced air of solemnity or sorrow. Laugh as we always laughed at the little jokes we enjoyed together. Play, smile, think of me, pray for me. Let my name be ever the household word that it always was. Let it be spoken without an effort, without the ghost of a shadow on it. Life means all that it ever meant. It is the same as it ever was; there is absolutely unbroken continuity. What is death but a negligible accident? I am but waiting for you, for an interval, somewhere very near, just around the corner. All is well.

From: *Facts of the Faith*, by Canon Scott Holland

I did not hear this magnificent exhortation to the family and friends of one who has recently died, until 1981. It expresses to me precisely the advice I would wish to give those nearest and dearest to me when my time comes. The words are so simple, the thought so clear, so wise and so kindly.

ANTONY HOPKINS C.B.E.
MUSICIAN, WRITER AND BROADCASTER

O you my fellow-men, who take me or denounce me for morose, crabbed, or misanthropical, how you do me wrong! you know not the secret cause of what seems thus to you. My heart and my disposition were from childhood up inclined to the tender feeling of goodwill, I was always minded to perform even great actions; but only consider that for six years past I have fallen into an incurable condition, aggravated by senseless physicians, year after year deceived in the hope of recovery, and in the end compelled to contemplate a *lasting malady*, the cure of which may take years or even prove impossible. Born with a fiery lively temperament, inclined even for the amusements of society, I was early forced to isolate myself to lead a solitary life. If now and again I tried for once to give the go-by to all this, O how rudely was I repulsed by the redoubled mournful experience of my defective hearing; but not yet could I bring myself to say to people 'Speak louder, shout, for I am deaf.' O how should I then bring myself to admit the weakness of *a sense* which ought to be more perfect in me than in others, a sense which I once possessed in the greatest perfection, a perfection such as few assuredly in my profession have yet possessed it in – O I cannot do it! forgive me then, if you see me shrink away when I would fain mingle among you. Double pain does my misfortune give me, in making me misunderstood. Recreation in human society, the more delicate passages of conversation, confidential outpourings, none of these are for me; all alone, almost only so much as the sheerest necessity demands can I bring myself to venture into society; I must live like an exile; if I venture into company a burning dread falls on me, the dreadful risk of letting my condition be perceived. So it was these last six months which I passed in the country, being ordered by my sensible physician to spare my hearing as much as possible. He fell in with what has now become almost my natural disposition, though sometimes, carried away by the craving for society, I let myself be misled into it; but what humiliation when someone stood by me and heard a flute in the distance, and *I* heard *nothing*, or when someone heard *the herd-boy singing*, and I again heard nothing. Such occurrences brought me nigh to despair, a little more and I had put an end to my own life – only it, *my art*, held me back. O it seemed to me impossible to quit the world until I had produced all I felt it in me to produce; and so I reprieved this wretched life – truly wretched, a body so sensitive that a change of any rapidity may alter my state from very good to very bad. Patience – that's the word, she it is I must take for my guide; I have done so – lasting I hope shall be my resolve to endure, till it please the inexorable Parcae to sever the thread. It may be things will go better, may be not; I am prepared – already in my twenty-eighth year forced – to turn philosopher: it is not easy, for an artist harder than for anyone. O God, Thou seest into my inward part, Thou art acquainted with it, Thou knowest that love to man and the inclination to beneficience dwell therein. O my fellowmen, when hereafter you read this, think that you have done me wrong; and the unfortunate, let him console himself by finding a companion in misfortune, who, despite all natural obstacles, has yet done everything in his power to take rank amongst good artists and good men. – You, my brothers Carl and   , as soon as I am dead, if Professor Schmidt is still alive, beg him in my name to describe my illness, and append this present document to his account in order that the world may at least as far as possible be reconciled with me after my death. – At the same time I appoint you both heirs to my little fortune (if so it may be styled); divide it fairly, and agree and help one another; what you have done against me has been, you well know, long since forgiven. You, brother Carl, I especially thank for the attachment you have shown me in this latter time. My wish is that you may have a better life with fewer cares than I have had; exhort your children to *virtue*, that alone can give happiness – not money, I speak from experience; that it was which upheld me even in misery, to that and to my art my thanks are due, that I did not end my life by suicide. – Farewell, and love each other. I send thanks to all my friends, especially *Prince Lichnowski* and *Professor Schmidt*. I want Prince L.'s instruments to remain in the safe keeping of one of you, but don't let there be any strife between you about it; only whenever they can help you to something more useful, sell them by all means. How glad am I if even under the sod I can be of use to you – so may it prove! With joy I hasten to meet death face to face. If he come before I have had opportunity to unfold all my artistic capabilities, he will, despite my hard fate, yet come too soon, and I no doubt should wish him later; but even then I am content; does he not free me from a state of ceaseless suffering? Come when thou wilt, I shall face thee with courage. Farewell, and do not quite forget me in death, I have deserved it of you, who in my life had often thought for you, for your happiness; may it be yours!

LUDWIG VAN BEETHOVEN.

Heiligenstadt,
   6th October, 1802.

   For my brothers
   Carl and
to be read and to execute after my death.
Heiligenstadt, *10th October*, 1802. So I take leave of thee – sad leave. Yes, the beloved hope that I brought here with me – at least in some degree to be cured – that hope must now altogether desert me. As the autumn leaves fall withered, so this hope too is for me withered up; almost as I came here, I go away. Even the lofty courage, which often in the lovely summer days animated me, has vanished. O Providence, let for once a pure day *of joy* be mine – so long already is true joy's inward resonance a stranger to me. O when, O when, O God, can I in the temple of Nature and of Humanity feel it once again. Never? No – O that were too cruel!

Testament, by Ludwig van Beethoven

I have chosen this not just for the obvious musical association but because it seems to tell us so much about Beethoven as a person. His image is indeed gruff, unapproachable, but here we have eloquent testimony that he fully realised this, and resented the mis-leading impression it gave of his true nature. Moreover these despairing words were written at just the time when he was composing one of his most delightful, exuberant and witty works, the Second Symphony, whose music seems a direct contradiction of the state of mind he describes in such pathetic terms. It seems that the document was never sent to the brothers to whom it is addressed and that therefore we may presume that the writing of it was a form of therapy, a facing-up to the inner self that he realised instinctively would be of benefit, long before psychoanalysis was invented.

MICHAEL HORDERN
ACTOR

Prospero: Now my charms are all o'erthrown,
And what strength I have 's mine own,
Which is most faint: now 'tis true
I must be here confin'd by you,
Or sent to Naples; let me not
Since I have my Dukedom got,
And pardon'd the deceiver, dwell
In this bare Island, by your spell,
But release me from my bands
With the help of your good hands:
Gentle breath of yours, my sails
Must fill, or else my project fails,
Which was to please: now I want
Spirits to enforce, Art to enchant:
And my ending is despair,
Unless I be reliev'd by prayer
Which pierces so, that it assaults
Mercy itself, and frees all faults.
    As you from crimes would pardon'd be,
    Let your indulgence set me free.
Exit

Epilogue to *The Tempest*, by William Shakespeare

I first felt the magic of *The Tempest* in 1952 when I played Caliban at Stratford; the following year I played Prospero at the Old Vic. In 1978 Prospero again, at Stratford, and then yet again for BBC television in 1980. Small wonder that I love the play.

When he comes to the matchless epilogue of *The Tempest* the actor is privileged to speak as Prospero saying goodbye to his island, as the actor of the last two hours saying good-bye to the empty stage behind him and lastly perhaps as William Shakespeare in his final play saying good-bye to the theatre and his public for ever. All in one speech. There's magic for you!

NICHOLAS HUMPHREY
PSYCHOLOGIST AND WRITER

Letter written on his second day at Westminster School, at the age of eleven.

MY DEAR DEAR MOTHER

If you don't let me come home, I die – I am all over ink, and my fine clothes have been spoilt – I have been tost in a blanket, and seen a ghost.

I remain, my dear dear Mother,

Your dutiful and most unhappy son,

FREDDY.

P.S. Remember me to my Father.

Frederick Reynolds, 1775, from: *Westminster*, by J. D. Carleton

Frederick Reynolds went on to become a minor playwright – an activity he recommended to his friends: 'Write a play – remember it is better to have written a damned play, than no play at all – it snatches a man from obscurity'. His own plays, alas, did not snatch him from obscurity. But this letter surely establishes him as one of the great Expressionist writers of his age.

CHRISTMAS HUMPHREYS
LAWYER

I hold that when a person dies
His soul returns again to earth;
Arrayed in some new flesh-disguise,
Another mother gives him birth.
With sturdier limbs and brighter brain
The old soul takes the roads again.

Such was my own belief and trust;
This hand, this hand that holds the pen,
Has many hundred times been dust
And turned, as dust, to dust again;
These eyes of mine have blinked and shone
In Thebes, in Troy, in Babylon.

All that I rightly think or do,
Or make, or spoil, or bless, or blast,
Is curse or blessing justly due
For sloth or effort in the past.
My life's a statement of the sum
Of vice indulged, or overcome.

I know that in my lives to be
My sorry heart will ache or burn
And worship, unavailingly,
The woman whom I used to spurn,
And shake to see another have
The love I spurned, the love she gave.

And I shall know, in angry words,
In gibes, in mocks, and many a tear,
A carrion flock of homing birds,
The gibes and scorns I uttered here;
The brave words that I failed to speak
Will brand me dastard on the cheek.

And as I wander on the roads
I shall be helped and healed and blessed;

Dear words shall cheer and be as goads
To urge to heights before unguessed.
My road shall be the road I made;
And all that I gave shall be repaid.

So shall I fight, so shall I tread,
In this long war beneath the stars;
So shall a glory wreathe my head,
So shall I faint and show the scars,
Until this case, this clogging mould,
Be smithied all to kingly gold.

'A Creed', by John Masefield

For the poet this poem was indeed a creed. He subscribed to *The Middle Way*, the journal of the Buddhist Society, and was keenly interested in Buddhism. The twin doctrines of Karma and Rebirth, the law of cause-effect and its working out in successive lives on earth, has been practised for thousands of years in the East, and is now becoming more and more known and accepted in the West. Truly our actions, wise and foolish, come home to us as 'a carrion flock of homing birds'. Even as all that we are, in body, mind and temperament is the product of past action, so shall we slowly rise 'to heights before unguessed' if, during this life, we create the causes which in lives to come will have this great effect.

There is in fact a good deal in English verse on this reasonable, just and noble doctrine. Tennyson, Browning, and Sir Edwin Arnold in *The Light of Asia* among others have all helped to make it known, but this is perhaps the finest poem as yet available to feed the heart and mind with this profoundly spiritual truth.

DAVID JACOBS
BROADCASTER

Miss J. Hunter Dunn, Miss J. Hunter Dunn,
Furnish'd and burnish'd by Aldershot sun,
What strenuous singles we played after tea,
We in the tournament – you against me!

Love-thirty, love-forty, oh! weakness of joy,
The speed of a swallow, the grace of a boy,
With carefullest carelessness, gaily you won,
I am weak from your loveliness, Joan Hunter Dunn.

Miss Joan Hunter Dunn, Miss Joan Hunter Dunn,
How mad I am, sad I am, glad that you won.
The warm-handled racket is back in its press,
But my shock-headed victor, she loves me no less.

Her father's euonymus shines as we walk,
And swing past the summer-house, buried in talk,
And cool the verandah that welcomes us in
To the six-o'clock news and a lime-juice and gin.

The scent of the conifers, sound of the bath,
The view from my bedroom of moss-dappled path,
As I struggle with double-end evening tie,
For we dance at the Golf Club, my victor and I.

On the floor of her bedroom lie blazer and shorts
And the cream-coloured walls are be-trophied with sports,
And westering, questioning settles the sun
On your low-leaded window, Miss Joan Hunter Dunn.

The Hillman is waiting, the light's in the hall,
The pictures of Egypt are bright on the wall,
My sweet, I am standing beside the oak stair
And there on the landing's the light on your hair.

By roads 'not adopted', by woodlanded ways,
She drove to the club in the late summer haze,
Into nine-o'clock Camberley, heavy with bells
And mushroomy, pine-woody, evergreen smells.

Miss Joan Hunter Dunn, Miss Joan Hunter Dunn,
I can hear from the car-park the dance has begun.
Oh! full Surrey twilight! importunate band!
Oh! strongly adorable tennis-girl's hand!

Around us are Rovers and Austins afar,
Above us, the intimate roof of the car,
And here on my right is the girl of my choice,
With the tilt of her nose and the chime of her voice,

And the scent of her wrap, and the words never said,
And the ominous, ominous dancing ahead,
We sat in the car park till twenty to one
And now I'm engaged to Miss Joan Hunter Dunn.

'A Subaltern's Love-Song', by Sir John Betjeman

I think I've always been a bit in love with Joan Hunter Dunn too!

CLIVE JAMES
WRITER

The sunlight on the garden
Hardens and grows cold,
We cannot cage the minute
Within its nets of gold,
When all is told
We cannot beg for pardon.

Our freedom as free lances
Advances towards its end;
The earth compels, upon it
Sonnets and birds descend;
And soon, my friend,
We shall have no time for dances.

The sky was good for flying
Defying the church bells
And every evil iron
Siren and what it tells:
The earth compels,
We are dying, Egypt, dying.

And not expecting pardon,
Hardened in heart anew,
But glad to have sat under
Thunder and rain with you,
And grateful too
For sunlight on the garden.

'The Sunlight on the Garden', by Louis MacNeice

Technically a magician, Louis MacNeice was too fastidiously classical a poet ever to let his verbal facility do his thinking for him. He always knew exactly what he meant. But along with the clear prose meaning that you can always extract from his poems goes a constant phonetic vitality that saturates thought with emotion, just as when the precise line of a drawing by Degas is filled in with pastel. One of the first modern poems I ever learned by heart, 'The Sunlight on the Garden', is one of my measures for how I would like my own writing to sound, if I was capable of MacNeice's clarity of thought together with his discriminating vividness of diction. Every phrase in the poem sounds like natural speech, even the one taken from 'Antony and Cleopatra'. Yet to assemble them all together in the one place and make the whole poem sound like natural speech took artifice of a high order. Above all it took a perfect ear, which where poets are concerned means the ability to hear words even when they are at work unspoken inside the brain. I have spoken this poem aloud many times, both in performance and to myself, but MacNeice need not necessarily have ever done so. If he had not been able to hear it accurately inside his head, he would never have been able to write it in the first place.

HUGH JOHNSON
AUTHOR AND WINE EXPERT

I

It was the winter wild,
While the heaven-born child
All meanly wrapt in the rude manger lies;
Nature, in awe to him,
Had doffed her gaudy trim,
With her great Master so to sympathize
It was no season then for her
To wanton with the Sun, her lusty paramour.

II

Only with speeches fair
She woos the gentle air
To hide her guilty front with innocent snow,
And on her naked shame,
Pollute with sinful blame,
The saintly veil of maiden white to throw;
Confounded, that her Maker's eyes
Should look so near upon her foul deformities.

III

But he, her fears to cease,
Sent down the meek-eyed Peace:
She, crowned with olive green, came softly sliding
Down through the turning sphere,
His ready harbinger,
With turtle wing the amorous clouds dividing;
And, waving wide her myrtle wand,
She strikes a universal peace through sea and land.

IV

No war, or battle's sound,
Was heard the world around;

The idle spear and shield were high uphung;
   The hooked chariot stood,
   Unstained with hostile blood;
The trumpet spake not to the armèd throng;
And kings sat still with awful eye,
As if they surely knew their sovran Lord was by.

V

   But peaceful was the night
   Wherein the Prince of Light
His reign of peace upon the earth began.
   The winds, with wonder whist,
   Smoothly the waters kissed,
Whispering new joys to the mild Ocean,
Who now hath quite forgot to rave,
While birds of calm sit brooding on the charmèd wave.

VI

   The stars, with deep amaze,
   Stand fixed in steadfast gaze,
Bending one way their precious influence,
   And will not take their flight,
   For all the morning light,
Or Lucifer that often warned them thence;
But in their glimmering orbs did glow,
Until their Lord himself bespake, and bid them go.

VII

   And, though the shady gloom
   Had given day her room,
The Sun himself withheld his wonted speed,
   And hid his head for shame,
   And his inferior flame
The new-enlightened world no more should need:
He saw a greater Sun appear
Than his bright throne or burning axletree could bear.

118

VIII

The shepherds on the lawn,
  Or ere the point of dawn,
Sat simply chatting in a rustic row;
  Full little thought they than
  That the mighty Pan
Was kindly come to live with them below:
  Perhaps their loves, or else their sheep,
Was all that did their silly thoughts so busy keep.

IX

When such music sweet
  Their hearts and ears did greet
As never was by mortal finger strook,
  Divinely-warbled voice
  Answering the stringed noise,
As all their souls in blissful rapture took:
  The air, such pleasure loth to lose,
With thousand echoes still prolongs each heavenly close.

From: 'Hymn on the Morning of Christ's Nativity',
by John Milton

I read this poem aloud to my family every Christmas. To me it shows more than any other the power of the simplest language to express even the most exalted and complicated thoughts and images. Milton wrote it in 1629. He could have used the sort of Latinized circumlocution that makes Paradise Lost such strange music. But for the elemental theme of Christmas and the birth of a child he knew that Anglo-Saxon words, especially monosyllables, have a power far beyond anything more exotic or artificial. Verse 8 is almost banal in its simplicity. But this is to make us see the shepherds, and hear the extraordinary music of verse 9 more clearly. The last line of verse 9 takes advantage of the stillness almost to play us the celestial chords themselves.

There is an introductory passage, starting 'This is the month, and this the happy morn ...' and there are eighteen more verses, but none with quite the magic of this opening to the Hymn.

BRIAN JOHNSTON
BROADCASTER

The scores were level and there were two wickets to fall. Silence fell. The gaffers, victims simultaneously of excitement and senility, could hardly raise their pint pots – for it was past 6 o'clock, and the front door of the Three Horse-shoes was now as wide open officially as the back door had been unofficially all afternoon.

The Major, his red face redder than ever and his chin sticking out almost as far as the Napoleonic Mr Ogilvy's, bowled a fast half-volley on the leg-stump. The sexton, a man of iron muscle from much digging, hit it fair and square in the middle of the bat, and it flashed like a thunderbolt, waist-high, straight at the youth in the blue jumper. With a shrill scream the youth sprang backwards out of its way and fell over on his back. Immediately behind him, so close were the fieldsmen clustered, stood the mighty Boone. There was no chance of escape for him. Even if he had possessed the figure and the agility to perform back-somersaults, he would have lacked the time. He had been unsighted by the youth in the jumper. The thunderbolt struck him in the midriff like a red-hot cannon-ball upon a Spanish galleon, and with the sound of a drumstick upon an insufficiently stretched drum. With a fearful oath, Boone clapped his hands to his outraged stomach and found that the ball was in the way. He looked at it for a moment in astonishment and then threw it down angrily and started to massage the injured spot while the field rang with applause at the brilliance of the catch.

Donald walked up and shyly added his congratulations. Boone scowled at him.

'I didn't want to catch the bloody thing,' he said sourly, massaging away like mad.

'But it may save the side,' ventured Donald.

'Blast the bloody side,' said Boone.

Donald went back to his place.

The scores were level and there was one wicket to fall. The last man in was the blacksmith, leaning heavily upon the shoulder of the baker, who was going to run for him, and limping as if in great pain. He took guard and looked round savagely. He was clearly still in a great rage.

The first ball he received he lashed at wildly and hit straight up in the air to an enormous height. It went up and up and up, until it became difficult to focus it properly against the deep, cloudless blue of the sky, and it carried with it the hopes and fears of an English village. Up and up it went and then at the top it seemed to hang motionless in the air, poised like a hawk, fighting, as it were, a heroic but forlorn battle against the chief invention of Sir Isaac Newton, and then it began its slow descent.

In the meanwhile things were happening below, on the terrestrial sphere. Indeed, the situation was rapidly becoming what the French call *mouvementé*. In the first place, the blacksmith forgot his sprained ankle and set out at a capital rate for the other end, roaring in a great voice as he went, 'Come on, Joe!' The baker, who was running on behalf of the invalid, also set out, and he also roared 'Come on, Joe!' and side by side, like a pair of high-stepping hackneys, the pair cantered along. From the other end Joe set out on his mission, and he roared 'Come on, Bill!' So all three came on. And everything would have been all right, so far as the running was concerned, had it not been for the fact that Joe, very naturally, ran with his head thrown back and his eyes goggling at the hawk-like cricket-ball. And this in itself would not have mattered if it had not been for the fact that the blacksmith and the baker, also very naturally, ran with their heads turned not only upwards but also backwards as well, so that they too gazed at the ball, with an alarming sort of squint and a truly terrific kink in their necks. Half-way down the pitch the three met with a magnificent clang, reminiscent of early, happy days in the tournament-ring at Ashby-de-la-Zouche, and the hopes of the village fell with the resounding fall of their three champions.

From: *England their England*, by A. G. MacDonnell

This short extract is from the description of the village cricket match which is quite simply the funniest thing ever written about cricket.

PETER JONES

ACTOR

Mr Bannister is the first low comedian on the stage. Let an author present him with a humorous idea, whether it be of jollity, of ludicrous distress, or of grave indifference, whether it be mock-heroic, burlesque, or mimicry, and he embodies it with an instantaneous felicity. No actor enters so well into the spirit of his audience as well as his author, for he engages your attention immediately by seeming to care nothing about you. The stage appears to be his own room, of which the audience compose the fourth wall: if they clap him, he does not stand still to enjoy their applause; he continues the action, if he cannot continue the dialogue; and this is the surest way to continue their applause. The stage is always supposed to be an actual room, or other scene, totally abstracted from an observant multitude, just like the room in which I am now scribbling: an actor, therefore, who indulges himself every moment in looking at the audience and acknowledging their approbation, is just as ridiculous as I should be myself, if I were to look every moment at the reflection of my own smiles in my looking-glass, or make a bow to the houses on the other side of the way.

From: *Dramatic Essays*, by Leigh Hunt

How would Jack Bannister cope with 'Sit-com' on television if he were alive to-day? Apart from the obvious disadvantage of being over two hundred years old, he would have a studio audience heard – but not seen – at home and be surrounded by cameras, microphones and scores of technicians going about their various tasks while he tried to remain absorbed in the scene and speak and listen to his fellow actors as though unobserved. It is said that the viewers at home cannot enjoy a show without accompanying laughter – often generated by an invited audience under an obligation to laugh and allowing themselves to be manipulated by a skilled 'WarmUp Man'. At other times his director would request him to pause at certain specified moments to allow laughter to be added at a later date (One series I did in England had a laugh track supplied by a firm in California, so viewers in Britain watched a comedy accompanied by laughter first generated by an audience watching some other show in Burbank, California!)

Judging from Leigh Hunt's beautifully observed description of his style, I think Bannister would have coped very well indeed.

In the beginning God didn't make just one or two people, he made a bunch of us. Because he wanted us to have a lot of fun and he said you can't really have fun unless there's a whole gang of you. So he put us all in this sort of playground park place called Eden and told us to enjoy.

At first we did have fun just like he expected. We played all the time. We rolled down the hills, waded in the streams, climbed the trees, swung on the vines, ran in the meadows, frolicked in the woods, hid in the forest, and acted silly. We laughed a lot.

Then one day this snake told us that we weren't having real fun because we weren't keeping score. Back then, we didn't know what score was. When he explained it, we still couldn't see the fun. But he said that we should give an apple to the person who was best at playing and we'd never know who was best unless we kept score. We could all see the fun of that. We were all sure we were best.

It was different after that. We yelled a lot. We had to make up new scoring rules for most of the games we played. Other games, like frolicking, we stopped playing because they were too hard to score. By the time God found out about our new fun, we were spending about forty-five minutes a day in actual playing and the rest of the time working out the score. God was wroth about that – very, very wroth. He said we couldn't use his garden anymore because we weren't having any fun. We said we were having lots of fun and we were. He shouldn't have got upset just because it wasn't exactly the kind of fun he had in mind.

He wouldn't listen. He kicked us out and said we couldn't come back until we stopped keeping score. To rub it in (to get our attention, he said), he told us we were all going to die anyway and our scores wouldn't mean anything.

He was wrong. My cumulative all-game score is now 16,548 and that means a lot to me. If I can raise it to 20,000 before I die I'll know I've accomplished something. Even if I can't my life has a great deal of meaning because I've taught my children to score high and they'll all be able to reach 20,000 or even 30,000 I know.

Really, it was life in Eden that didn't mean anything. Fun is great in its place, but without scoring there's no reason for it. God has a very superficial view of life and I'm glad my children are being raised away from his influence. We were lucky to get out. We're all very grateful to the snake.

'Snake', by Anne Herbert

Humour is so important in my work as a psychotherapist. This piece makes me laugh. When we human beings were a more primitive species we probably had more fun. Now we crawl all over each other, shoot guns and bombs trying to achieve 'success', and for many life is one great stress.

I have treated many children who couldn't read or who had lost the ability to speak. They rarely lose the ability to laugh and have fun, which is a good way back into expression.

BRUCE KENT

GENERAL SECRETARY: CAMPAIGN FOR NUCLEAR DISARMAMENT

These few words are being set down here as they come from my mind and my heart. And if I must write them with my hands in chains, I find that much better than if my will were in chains ...

For us men there are only two possibilities in this world: either we become ever better or ever worse; there is simply no such thing as standing still. Yes, even for those who have worked hard to come closer to God, there can be many reverses, just as an army advancing towards its victory does not win all its battles but must endure many defeats. Nevertheless, this does not mean that the struggle should be given up as hopeless; instead, one must pick himself up with renewed strength and strive on again towards the desired goals ...

You must love God, your Lord, and your neighbour as yourself. On these two commandments rests the whole law ... Many actually believe quite simply that things have to be the way they are. If this should happen to mean that they are obliged to commit injustice, then they believe that others are responsible. The oath would not be a lie for someone who believes he can go along and is willing to do so. But if I know in advance that I cannot accept and obey everything I would promise under that oath, then I would be guilty of a lie. For this reason I am convinced that it is still best that I speak the truth, even if it costs me my life. For you will not find it written in any of the commandments of God or of the Church, that a man is obliged under pain of sin to take an oath committing him to obey whatever might be commanded of him by his secular ruler ...

Dear wife, forgive me everything by which I have grieved or offended you. For my part, I have forgiven everything. Ask all those in Radegund whom I have ever injured or offended to forgive me too.

Franz Jagerstatter, quoted in: *In Solitary Witness*,
by Gordon Zahn

I hope that you will find this extract from a Last Letter as moving as I do. It was written in a prison in Berlin in the summer of 1943 by an Austrian farmer, Franz Jagerstatter, to his wife shortly before his death as a criminal. It is one of the miracles of history that his name and story were not lost in the tumult of the great calamities of the Second World War. You can read the full account in a book called *In Solitary Witness* by Gordon Zahn, who spent many months after that war gathering together the different strands of the Jagerstatter story.

Franz Jagerstatter was a simple man, direct and honest, without secondary education. Happily married, he was the father of three little girls, and the sacristan of the village church. As Hitler's armies needed more and more men, he was called to fight in the February of 1943. Despite 'good' advice from church, family and friends, Franz knew that he could take no part in a war which he judged to be unjust and cruel. It would be impossible for him to take the military oath of obedience. So, alone, he refused military service. For such a refusal there was only one punishment.

After many months of imprisonment, with only his wonderful faith to support him, he was finally sentenced to death, and on 9 August 1943 he was beheaded in that Berlin prison.

For me he is the symbol of the small man who has the courage to say 'No', despite the consequences, to the endless demands of the nation state which expects such conformity from us all.

His ashes now lie in the graveyard of the little village church of St Radegund a few kilometres from the German border. The Parish Priest has added Franz's name to the list of dead on the war memorial with the additional phrase 'he also died a hero'.

A much wider world now realises that Franz Jagerstatter, in his life and death, showed us a heroism and a vision which we have all in our different ways to imitate if we are to survive in this war-like world, and to turn it into a real community of peoples.

DAVID KOSSOFF
WRITER AND ACTOR

Lord – you have a minute?
This is a little important. I've been
   meaning to bring this up for some
   weeks, but you know, this and that ...
It's on behalf of shy children.
I was one, and my eldest is one.
My wife is still one. So's my
   married sister – and my friend Lou.
Lou says to be shy is to remain a
   child in the most painful way.
No fool, Lou.

But let's stay with children, Lord.
Shy grown-ups can cope; in various ways.
   A person learns how. How to
   build the various walls for
   hiding behind. A person learns.
But children, Lord. They have it rough.
And they are surrounded by grown-ups
   who, in the main, don't understand.
Or have forgotten, behind their walls,
   the Hell it can be.

I've read learned bits by educated parties
   positively proving that shy ones
   are made, not born.
Or is it born, not made?
You think it makes any difference, Lord?
You think it's comfort, Lord?
You think it helps a head-bent,
   tongue-tied, blushing, speechless kid?
Like a second head it helps.
Like a third leg.

You should excuse me, Lord,
   but a person could get puzzled.

I'll try to explain.
    A grown-up misbehaves; does wrong;
    breaks one of your ten rules.
You find a way to teach him a lesson, to
    punish him a little.
It's your way; justice with mercy.
Good system. Tried and trusted.

The punishments are graded; as is right.
Ranging from a little slap for a
    little sin to real Hell for a big 'un.
Real Hell. Something as bad as, for
    instance, suddenly making a
    person shy.
Not grown-up shy; with walls.
Shy like a child.
That's real Hell, Lord. Ask a shy child.

So why children, Lord?
Punishment in advance?
Doesn't seem like you – and shy
    people are *less* likely to get into
    big trouble, am I right?
So why children, Lord?
What's the *point* of shyness?
Modesty, yes, sense of proportion, yes.
Quietness, respect for others, yes.
But shyness?
Tongue-locked, brain-blocked,
Turned-in, turned off,
Eye-lowered, head-lowered *Hell*?

Forgive me, Lord, I always seem
    to be raising my voice.
But you are busy; a lot to look after,
    and perhaps things get overlooked.
I don't know how good your staff is.
    (Angels strike me as decorative
    rather than useful. I may be
    wrong. Bit unworldly they seem.)

So things perhaps are not brought
   to your attention.
Well, Lord, you yourself invented the
   way to bring things to your attention,
And called it prayer.
This is a prayer, dear Friend,
   on behalf of shy children.

'Shy Children', by David Kossoff

When this 'prayer' was done on television, once in a series of my
own, and on another occasion as a guest, it brought many letters
of an 'Oh, me too!' kind. Included in a one-man show or
luncheon talk, similar involvement can be sensed, often heard.
What a puzzlement is shyness . . .

CLEO LAINE
SINGER

How prosperous is this good prince!
The goodly destiny has come to pass,
The Generations pass away,
While others remain,
Since the time of the ancestors,
The gods who were aforetime,
Who rest in their pyramids,
Nobles and the glorious likewise departed,
Entombed in these pyramids ...

Behold the places thereof:
Their walls are dismantled,
Their places are no more,
As if they had never been.

None cometh from thence
That he may tell us how they fare,
That he may tell us of their fortunes,
That he may content our heart,
Until we too depart
To the place whither they have gone.

Encourage thy heart to forget it,
Making it pleasant for thee to follow thy desire,
Whilst thou livest.
Put myrrh on thy head,
And garments on thee of fine linen
Imbued with marvellous luxuries,
The genuine things of the gods.

Increase yet more thy delights
And let (not) thy heart languish.
Follow thy desire and thy good,
Fashion thine affairs on earth
After the mandates of thy own heart.
Till that day of lamentation cometh to thee,
When the silent-hearted hears not thy lamentation,
Nor he that is in the tomb attends the mourning.

Celebrate the glad day,
Be not weary therein,
Lo, no man taketh his goods with him.
Yea, none returneth again that is gone thither.

'Song of the Harp Player', from:
The Oriental Philosophers – An Introduction, by
E. W. F. Tomlin

I was reading this poem when I received the request to send something. I could have selected other poems and might have done, had I not thought this one was so appropriate.

It was written in 2,200 BC or thereabouts – one of the first poems to be recorded – I felt amazement as I read it, and was moved immensely.

KENNETH LAMBERT
JUNGIAN ANALYST

In the most unexpected quarters nowadays we find people who can no longer blink the fact that something ought to be done about man in regard to his psychology. Unfortunately, the word 'ought' tells us that they do not know what to do, and do not know the way that leads to the goal. We can, of course, hope for the undeserved grace of God, who hears our prayers. But God, who also does *not* hear our prayers, wants to become man, and for that purpose he has chosen, through the Holy Ghost, the creaturely man filled with darkness – the natural man who is tainted with original sin and who learnt the divine arts and sciences from the fallen angels. The guilty man is eminently suitable and is therefore chosen to become the vessel for the continuing incarnation, not the guiltless one who holds aloof from the world and refuses to pay his tribute to life, for in him the dark God would find no room. Since the Apocalypse, we now know again that God is not only to be loved, but also to be feared.

The religious need longs for wholeness, and therefore lays hold of the images of wholeness offered by the unconscious, which, independently of the conscious mind, rise up from the depths of our psychic nature.

The question as to whether the process of integration is initiated by consciousness or by the archetype can never be answered; unless, in contradiction to experience, one either robbed the archetype of its autonomy or degraded consciousness to a mere machine. We find ourselves in best agreement with psychological experience if we concede to the archetype a definite measure of independence, and to consciousness a degree of creative freedom proportionate to its scope. There then arises that reciprocal action between two relatively autonomous factors which compels us, when describing and explaining the processes, to present sometimes the one and sometimes the other factor as the acting subject even when God becomes man. The Christian solution has hitherto avoided this difficulty by recognising Christ as the one and only God-man. But the indwelling of the Holy Ghost, the third Divine Person, in man, brings about a

Christification of many, and the question then arises whether these many are all complete God-men. Such a transformation would lead to insufferable collisions between them, to say nothing of the unavoidable inflation to which the ordinary mortal, who is not freed from original sin, would instantly succumb. In these circumstances it is well to remind ourselves of St Paul and his split consciousness; on one side he felt that he was the apostle directly called and enlightened by God, and, on the other side, a sinful man who could not pluck out the 'thorn in the flesh' and rid himself of the Satanic angel who plagued him. That is to say, even the enlightened person remains what he is, and is never more than his own limited ego before the One who dwells in him, whose form has no knowable boundaries, who encompasses him on all sides fathomless as the abysms of the earth and vast as the sky.

From 'Answer to Job', in: *Psychology and Religion*, part I, VI, by C. G. Jung

I deeply respect the way in which, for many people of this century, Jung's work proposes discoveries and considerations in the field of Psychology and Religion that merit a response from the depths of the individual psyche and a consideration of the extent to which, from the angle of consciousness, we are very much less the masters of our fate than our hubristic pretensions may find it easy to tolerate. There are, common to mankind, dynamic structures and processes, arising from within the psyche, which we fail to come to terms with at our urgent peril – though it needs be in the uniquely creative way that belongs to the potential of every individual. However paradoxical it may seem, it remains that the universal patterns of potentiality that are designated archetypal by Jung, and are the means by which experience is ordered and shaped for us, even through us, may be understood as willy nilly part of our basic structure. As a consequence, in a way, we 'create' a world that is individual to us and yet also discover the extent to which the human life that is shared by all men is the resultant of confrontations and struggles arising out of a long-drawn-out dialectic within the historical process. This dialectic turns out to be between ego-consciousness and unconscious potential; between our 'good' intentions and the shadow opposite of them that remains perilously unconscious; between masculine and feminine counterpoles; between the past and the present; between psyche and soma. Within the process of the integration of the many parts and levels of the personality, deintegrations for the purpose of making way for new experience and then reintegrations continuously succeed each other. These processes can be frequent and progressive, and creative if we can maintain conscious collaboration with them, but they may produce disastrous consequences if we refuse consciousness to them through fear or anger.

Jung's contributions have helped me personally to understand better the holistic imagery and symbolism, the poetry indeed, that arises spontaneously both within the individual and within our collective religious, mythological and cultural heritages. To neglect this is to be open to danger, for, as Jung reminds us, 'God is not only to be loved but also to be feared' as befits a Being that may be designated as a combination of opposites, rather than as one-sidedly 'good' as could seem so desirable judged from our limited point of view. We are being afforded an opportunity both as individuals and as societies, not only to rediscover and find meaning afresh in, for instance, that symbolic content of religion that for many people feels so dead, but also to become aware of as yet undiscovered aspects of it that can modify and clarify some of the difficulties and paradoxes, inherent in it, that cause trouble, if not confusion, in a multitude of reflective people.

MARGHANITA LASKI
WRITER AND BROADCASTER

From our low seat beside the fire
  Where we have dozed and dreamed and watched the glow
Or raked the ashes, stooping so
We scarcely saw the sun or rain
  Above, or looked much higher
Than this same quiet red or burned-out fire.
      To-night we heard a call,
      A rattle on the window-pane,
      A voice on the sharp air,
And felt a breath stirring our hair,
  A flame within us: Something swift and tall
  Swept in and out and that was all.
Was it a bright or a dark angel? Who can know?
  It left no mark upon the snow,
    But suddenly it snapped the chain,
    Unbarred, flung wide the door
    Which will not shut again;
  And so we cannot sit here any more.
    We must arise and go:
    The world is cold without
    And dark and hedged about
  With mystery and enmity and doubt.
    But we must go
    Though yet we do not know
Who called, or what marks we shall leave upon the snow.

            'The Call', by Charlotte Mew

This is one of the later – I think one of the very best – poems
by Charlotte Mew who lived from 1869 to 1928 when she killed
herself, a tragic woman throughout a life that was dogged by loneliness and terror of hereditary insanity. She was at her best, as here,
a great poet. It would, I think, be crass to try to say anything very
precise about the 'meaning' of this poem, for its ambiguities
reverberate in such richness that almost everyone could write his
or her own needs into it. To me its most potent force is in what
it seems to say about the duties imposed, for better and for worse,
by inspiration.

BERNARD LEVIN
JOURNALIST AND AUTHOR

Xenophon and the rearguard heard it and thought that there were some more enemies attacking in the front, since there were natives of the country they had ravaged following them up behind, and the rearguard had killed some of them and made prisoners of others in an ambush, and captured about twenty raw ox-hide shields, with the hair on. However, when the shouting got louder and drew nearer, and those who were constantly going forward started running towards the men in front who kept on shouting, and the more there were of them the more shouting there was, it looked then as though this was something of considerable importance. So Xenophon mounted his horse and, taking Lycus and the cavalry with him, rode forward to give support, and, quite soon, they heard the soldiers shouting out 'The sea! The sea!' and passing the word down the column. Then certainly they all began to run, the rearguard and all, and drove on the baggage animals and the horses at full speed; and when they had all got to the top, the soldiers, with tears in their eyes, embraced each other and their generals and captains. In a moment, at somebody or other's suggestion, they collected stones and made a great pile of them. On top they put a lot of raw ox-hides and staves and the shields which they had captured.

From: *Anabasis*, by Xenophon (translated by Rex Warner)

This has always seemed to me one of the great moments of history, and the description of it among the most moving passages I know in any language. At the beginning of the fourth century BC, a Greek army had been raised on behalf of Cyrus, pretender to the throne of Persia; the Greeks had marched a thousand miles, with only a handful of cavalry, and were almost at the gates of Babylon. Then, at the Battle of Cunaxa, though the Greeks were victorious in their sector, Cyrus was killed, and the entire purpose of the expedition had disappeared. Moreover, all the Greek leaders, tricked by the offer of a safe-conduct, were massacred by the Persians. The army was in despair, but Xenophon's hour had come. He rallied the Greeks and accepted – with genuine reluctance – the command.

The march of the Ten Thousand (though fewer than half survived) followed, and Xenophon led them, through constant hardship and danger, back to the homes they had given up hope of ever seeing again. The passage describes their arrival on the shores of the Black Sea, from which, though they still had hundreds of miles to go, they knew they could get back to Greece. Xenophon, incidentally, writes of himself in the third person; of how many modern generals' memoirs can that be said?

EARL OF LONGFORD K.G., P.C.

Because I do not hope to turn again
Because I do not hope
Because I do not hope to turn
Desiring this man's gift and that man's scope
I no longer strive to strive towards such things
(Why should the agèd eagle stretch its wings?)
Why should I mourn
The vanished power of the usual reign?

Because I do not hope to know again
The infirm glory of the positive hour
Because I do not think
Because I know I shall not know
The one veritable transitory power
Because I cannot drink
There, where trees flower, and springs flow, for there is
    nothing again

Because I know that time is always time
And place is always and only place
And what is actual is actual only for one time
And only for one place
I rejoice that things are as they are and
I renounce the blessèd face
And renounce the voice
Because I cannot hope to turn again
Consequently I rejoice, having to construct something

Upon which to rejoice
And pray to God to have mercy upon us
And I pray that I may forget
These matters that with myself I too much discuss
Too much explain
Because I do not hope to turn again
Let these words answer
For what is done, not to be done again
May the judgement not be too heavy upon us

Because these wings are no longer wings to fly
But merely vans to beat the air
The air which is now thoroughly small and dry
Smaller and dryer that the will
Teach us to care and not to care
Teach us to sit still.

Pray for us sinners now and at the hour of our death
Pray for us now and at the hour of our death.

From: Ash Wednesday, by T. S. Eliot

I have selected these lines because of their message. They are
beautiful, it seems to me, in themselves, but the message is the most
important, and the most difficult, that in this life we have to learn.

Titty outside and Dick inside the pigeon-loft were waiting for the first of the returning pigeons. Dick was finding it hard to keep his mind on gold. He never had been able to think of two things at once. He laid *Phillips on Metals* aside and had yet another look at the pigeons' own front door. It was oblong, with a slide that closed either one half or the other. When the slide was pushed to the right the pigeons could go freely in or out. When it was pushed to the left it left an opening with a row of wires hung on a bar. A strip of wood on the threshold stopped them from swinging outwards, but a pigeon coming in could push through them, and as soon as it was inside they would fall back into place. Carefully, with a finger, Dick lifted two or three of the little swinging wires through which the pigeons had to push their way. They were very light. Everything would depend on the pigeons' strength and eagerness. Did they simply crash in, or did they feel their way in timidly, so that any little extra weight would stop them from wanting to come in at all? Titty was on the steps outside the loft, steep wooden steps up out of the old stableyard, keeping watch to warn Dick of the coming of the first pigeon. From there she could look out over the low outbuildings, and the shrubs and little trees beyond them to the hills on the further side of the river, and, in the distance to the great mass of Kanchenjunga, brown and blue and purple, rising into the dazzling brightness of the summer sky. Somewhere up there, under the blazing sun, John, Susan and Nancy, pioneers, were exploring on behalf of the Company. Sounds of painters and plasterers at work, the moving of ladders and furniture, whistling and laughter, came from the house. But the noise of hammering and sawing came not from the house but from the camp in the garden, where Peggy and Roger were finishing the sleeping hutch for Timothy. Every now and then Dorothea came running into the yard to get more nails or screws from the old stable under the pigeon-loft where Captain Flint had a carpenter's bench.

Homer was in the yard before ever Titty saw him. Her eyes were almost blind with staring into the sky, trying to see a black speck that would come nearer and nearer, bigger and bigger, and turn at last into a pigeon. But she never saw how Homer came. Suddenly there was the fluttering of wings, and Homer was already in the yard, flying uncertainly from house roof to stable roof, puzzled, perhaps, by the sight of Titty sitting on the steps.

'Dick,' called Titty softly.

There was no answer.

The pigeon flew across towards the loft.

'Dick,' cried Titty, desperate. 'He's here.'

She heard a low murmur, 'Go and tell Peggy.'

The next moment Homer had lighted on the narrow shelf, stretched and closed his wings, and pushed his way in under the swinging wires which lifted to let him pass.

'News from the wilderness', from: *Pigeon Post*, by Arthur Ransome

When I was about nine years old I had to spend several weeks flat on my back in bed after a car accident, trussed up in a leather and steel embrace, and my only real pleasure, though I felt more fed up than uncomfortable, was reading. Someone produced an odd device like an upside-down lectern which allowed me to read books through a piece of transparent plastic, and I must have devoured almost a volume a day. The ones I enjoyed most, though I was not a sporty child and didn't know one end of a sailing dinghy from another, were Arthur Ransome's *Swallows and Amazons* books, set mostly in the English Lake District. I think there were about a dozen of them, and each seemed satisfyingly long. None of my friends shared my delight in them, which probably made them even more exclusively enjoyable. At any rate I know that years later, when I was sorting out my childhood books, I was aghast to find that only *Pigeon Post* remained. It's from this that I've chosen an extract.

BARBARA MARKHAM
ACTRESS AND VOICE AND DRAMA COACH

Out of us all
That make rhymes,
Will you choose
Sometimes –
As the winds use
A crack in a wall
Or a drain,
Their joy or their pain
To whistle through –
Choose me,
You English words?

I know you:
You are light as dreams,
Tough as oak,
Precious as gold,
As poppies and corn,
Or an old cloak:
Sweet as our birds
To the ear,
As the burnet rose
In the heat
Of Midsummer:
Strange as the races
Of dead and unborn:
Strange and sweet
Equally,
And familiar,
To the eye,
As the dearest faces
That a man knows,
And as lost homes are:

But though older far
Than oldest yew, –
As our hills are, old, –
Worn new

Again and again:
Young as our streams
After rain:
And as dear
As the earth which you prove
That we love.

Make me content
With some sweetness
From Wales
Whose nightingales
Have no wings, –
From Wiltshire and Kent
And Herefordshire,
And the villages there, –
From the names, and the things
No less.
Let me sometimes dance
With you,
Or climb
Or stand perchance
In ecstasy,
Fixed and free
In a rhyme,
As poets do.

'Words', by Edward Thomas

Edward Thomas communicated so much in so few words. In this extremely beautiful poem, his appeal for the English words he so loved, he helps us to understand his own feelings about those words with their sounds and their limitless significance in a way which ordinary mortals long to be able to do, but can't. At least we can experience the joy of language through reading him.

IAN McEWAN

WRITER

An Italian author – Giulio Cordara, a Jesuit – has written a
poem upon insects, which he begins by insisting, that those
troublesome and abominable little animals were created for
our annoyance, and that they were certainly not inhabitants
of Paradise. We of the north may dispute this piece of
theology; but on the other hand, it is clear as the snow on the
house-tops, that Adam was not under the necessity of
shaving; and that when Eve walked out of her delicious
bower, she did not step upon ice three inches thick.

Some people say it is a very easy thing to get up of a cold
morning. You have only, they tell you, to take the resolution;
and the thing is done. This may be very true; just as a boy
at school has only to take a flogging, and the thing is over. But
we have not at all made up our minds upon it; and we find
it a very pleasant exercise to discuss the matter, candidly,
before we get up. This at least is not idling, though it may be
lying. It affords an excellent answer to those, who ask how
lying in bed can be indulged in by a reasoning being, – a
rational creature. How? Why, with the argument calmly at
work in one's head, and the clothes over one's shoulder.
Oh – it is a fine way of spending a sensible, impartial half-
hour.

If these people would be more charitable, they would get
on with their argument better. But they are apt to reason so
ill, and to assert so dogmatically, that one could wish to have
them stand round one's bed of a bitter morning, and lie
before their faces. They ought to hear both sides of the bed,
the inside and out. If they cannot entertain themselves with
their own thoughts for half an hour or so, it is not the fault
of those who can. If their will is never pulled aside by the
enticing arms of imagination, so much the luckier for the
stage-coachman.

Candid inquiries into one's decumbency, besides the
greater or less privileges to be allowed a man in proportion
to his ability of keeping early hours, the work given his
faculties, etc., will at least concede their due merits to such
representations as the following. In the first place, says the

injured but calm appealer, I have been warm all night, and find my system in a state perfectly suitable to a warm-blooded animal. To get out of this state into the cold, besides the inharmonious and uncritical abruptness of the transition, is so unnatural to such a creature, that the poets, refining upon the tortures of the damned, make one of their greatest agonies consist in being suddenly transported from heat to cold, – from fire to ice. They are 'haled' out of their 'beds', says Milton, by 'harpy-footed furies', – fellows who come to call them. On my first movement towards the anticipation of getting up, I find that such parts of the sheets and bolster, as are exposed to the air of the room, are stone-cold. On opening my eyes, the first thing that meets them is my own breath rolling forth, as if in the open air, like smoke out of a cottage chimney. Think of this symptom. Then I turn my eyes sideways and see the window all frozen over. Think of that. Then the servant comes in. 'It is very cold this morning, is it not?' – 'Very cold, Sir.' – 'Very cold indeed, isn't it?' – 'Very cold indeed, Sir.' – 'More than usually so, isn't it, even for this weather?' (Here the servant's wit and good-nature are put to a considerable test, and the inquirer lies on thorns for the answer.) 'Why, Sir ... I think it *is*.' (Good creature! There is not a better, or more truth-telling servant going.) 'I must rise, however, – get me some warm water.' – Here comes a fine interval between the departure of the servant and the arrival of the hot water; during which, of course, it is of 'no use' to get up. The hot water comes. 'Is it quite hot?' – 'Yes, Sir.' – 'Perhaps too hot for shaving: I must wait a little?' – 'No, Sir; it will just do.' (There is an over-nice propriety sometimes, an officious zeal of virtue, a little troublesome.) 'Oh – the shirt – you must air my clean shirt; – linen gets very damp this weather.' – 'Yes, Sir.' Here another delicious five minutes. A knock at the door. 'Oh, the shirt – very well. My stockings – I think the stockings had better be aired too.' – 'Very well, Sir.' – Here another interval.

From: 'Getting up on Cold Mornings', by Leigh Hunt

Politicians like to boast that they are up by 5.00 am doing press-ups and attending to affairs of state.

The world might be a safer, gentler place if they could be persuaded to stay in bed a little longer, and I offer this extract from Leigh Hunt's civilised essay as a contribution to world peace.

ROGER McGOUGH
POET

I do not smile because I am happy.
Because I gurgle I am not content.
I feel in colours, mottled, mainly black.
And the only sound I hear is the sea
Pounding against the white cliffs of my skull.

For seven months I lay in a coma.
Agony.
Darkness.
My screams drowned by the wind
Of my imperceptible breathing.

One morning the wind died down. I awoke.

You are with me now as you are everyday
Seeking some glimmer of recognition
Some sign of recovery. You take my hand.
I try to say: 'I love you.'
Instead I squawk,
Eyes bobbing like dead birds in a watertank.
I try to say: 'Have pity on me, pity on yourself
Put a bullet between the birds.'
Instead I gurgle.
You kiss me then walk out of the room.
I see your back.
I feel a colour coming, mottled, mainly black.

'Head Injury', from *After the Merrymaking*, by Roger
McGough

I was moved some years ago, by a programme on television that had
been filmed in a Birmingham Hospital. There was a ward devoted
to young men who had been involved in motor-cycle accidents,
many of whom were on life-support systems. The idea of being in
a coma, with perhaps a frustrated consciousness trapped inside a
useless body, is the central theme of the poem.

A secondary theme is one that lies below many of my poems, and that is, the difficulty we have in communicating, often with those nearest to us.

IAN McKELLEN
ACTOR

THE LEADEN ECHO

How to kéep – is there ány any, is there none such, nowhere
    known some, bow or brooch or braid or brace, láce,
    latch or catch or key to keep
Back beauty, keep it, beauty, beauty, beauty, ... from
    vanishing away?
Ó is there no frowning of these wrinkles, rankèd wrinkles
    deep,
Dówn? no waving off of these most mournful messengers,
    still messengers, sad and stealing messengers of grey? –
No there's none, there's none, O no there's none,
Nor can you long be, what you now are, called fair,
Do what you may do, what, do what you may,
And wisdom is early to despair:
Be beginning; since, no, nothing can be done
To keep at bay   10
Age and age's evils, hoar hair,
Ruck and wrinkle, drooping, dying, death's worst, winding
    sheets, tombs and worms and tumbling to decay;
So be beginning, be beginning to despair.
O there's none; no no no there's none:
Be beginning to despair, to despair,
Despair, despair, despair, despair.

THE GOLDEN ECHO

Spare!
There ís one, yes I have one (Hush there!),
Only not within seeing of the sun.
Not within the singeing of the strong sun,
Tall sun's tingeing, or treacherous the tainting of the earth's
    air,
Somewhere elsewhere there is ah well where! one,
Óne. Yes I cán tell such a key, I dó know such a place,

Where whatever's prizèd and passes of us, everything that's
    fresh and fast flying of us, seems to us sweet of us and
    swiftly away with, done away with, undone,
Undone, done with, soon done with, and yet dearly and
    dangerously sweet
Of us, the wimpled-water-dimpled, not-by-morning-
    matchèd face,   10
The flower of beauty, fleece of beauty, too too apt to, ah! to
    fleet,
Never fleets móre, fastened with the tenderest truth
To its own best being and its loveliness of youth: it is an ever-
    lastingness of, O it is an all youth!
Come then, your ways and airs and looks, locks, maidengear,
    gallantry and gaiety and grace,
Winning ways, airs innocent, maiden manners, sweet looks,
    loose locks, long locks, lovelocks, gaygear, going gallant,
    girlgrace –
Resign them, sign them, seal them, send them, motion them
    with breath,
And with sighs soaring, soaring síghs, deliver
Them; beauty-in-the-ghost, deliver it, early now, long before
    death
Give beauty back, beauty, beauty, beauty, back to God,
    beauty's self and beauty's giver.
See; not a hair is, not an eyelash, not the least lash lost; every
    hair   20
Is, hair of the head, numbered.

Nay, what we had lighthanded left in surly the mere mould
Will have waked and have waxed and have walked with the
    wind what while we slept,
This side, that side hurling a heavyheaded hundredfold
What while we, while we slumbered.
O then, weary then whý should we tread? O why are we so
    haggard at the heart, so care-coiled, care-killed, so fagged,
    so fashed, so cogged, so cumbered,
When the thing we freely fórfeit is kept with fonder a care,
Fonder a care kept than we could have kept it, kept
Far with fonder a care (and we, we should have lost it) finer,
    fonder
A care kept. – Where kept? do but tell us where kept, where. –

Yonder. – What high as that! We follow, now we follow. –
    Yonder, yes yonder, yonder,
Yonder.

'The Leaden Echo and the Golden Echo', by Gerard Manley
Hopkins

On the page, G. M. Hopkins' poetry can seem too dense for the
reader to understand. But as soon as they are read aloud, his words
leap out at you, spontaneous where they had perhaps seemed
merely literary, even archaic; now glistening like jewels. 'The
Leaden Echo' and 'The Golden Echo' were intended for some sort
of performance; they are a chorus for an unfinished play. They
remind me of Shakespeare's late verse, in *The Winter's Tale*, for
example.

'The Leaden Echo' is all mournful; the rhythms get slower and
slower until the final word, five times repeated. Then with a simple
pun, the rhythm hesitates, the sun shines out and the words of 'The
Golden Echo' race on to their climax. How I wish Hopkins had
completed his play! No-one was more fitted to revive the glory of
Elizabethan dramatic poetry.

YEHUDI MENUHIN
MUSICIAN AND WRITER

Like hot ice, cold and smouldering
he lay in his brother's damp, suburban house,
knocking on the wall. The fever crowned him
and Vienna never seemed as far again,
when the ugly little pianist in *The Green Anchor*
drove the dancers like a drunken cabby
into that glittering afternoon where waltzes
composed themselves, everybody was in tune
and melody caught at the heart's high points
swaying like a steeplejack. He was what friends sang
for their suppers, the menu they ate their way through,
ending sweet-toothed with the Erl-King played on a comb.

He went down as well as new wine
at *The Blue Hedgehog*, among encores of empty glasses,
always believing a good boy should amount to more.
Seven good masses went straight up to heaven
and were never heard of again. In a few late salons
three dukes kissed his patron and declared his music
heavenly as angels, bellies slung like bows,
fleethaired and trumpeting, gilded on a weathervane
and as high above him, tubby among the Biedermeier.
Somewhere Weber was drowning his operas like puppies.
But the funeral march always finished in a happy wake,
the faithful would stand a round
and Lazarus sat up singing.

Money and the seasons were against him.
Even so, he fell on the smallest poems, unerring as rain
and the beergardens heard them opening like operas.
In that grudging spring when publishers fruit
he had florins like blackberries.

Sweet Gusti's love, which chased him three times
around St Peter's Church, he finished by denying;
but there was no end to loving women
and more ways than Metternich had spies.

The cure, he found, took a fiercer hold —
love left him understanding that nothing
eats hair like mercury. He struggled out of the poxy dark
pale and almost bald, good mushroom he was, still singing.

Psalms for the cantor, jingles for the choir,
back to school in fugue and counterpoint,
respectability like a pious accountant imploring him
to drown birdsong in thunder and God
would appoint the cabby *Kapellmeister*.
Always expecting something like this, his music prepared
to carry on without him. Inside his skull, tough as a chipped
    cup
the scores were adding up, so many even Beethoven blinked
and lay back humming like a top.
All stopped in a wintry corner under the earth.
Above him the snow was laying itself out like linen
but somewhere deep inside there was spring
and he ended, knocking on the wall, crying to be let in.

   'Schubert at Wieden', by Christopher Hope

Schubert, quite simply, was the first composer to be humanly
himself. Defenceless, poor and unprotected, this rather ordinary
young man of undistinguished appearance became through his
music the very incarnation of mortal pain and human courage.
Schubert died having never heard his great symphonies. Yet he
speaks in a voice of such joy, such gaiety, that the truth of life,
comic and tragic, is brought home to us. And he had an extraordinary gift for transforming poems into music. What I like about
this poem is that it transforms Schubert into poetry.

JONATHAN MILLER

When God at first made man,
Having a glasse of blessings standing by;
Let us (said he) poure on him all we can:
Let the worlds riches, which dispersed lie,
   Contract into a span.

So strength first made a way;
Then beautie flow'd, then wisdome, honour, pleasure:
When almost all was out, God made a stay,
Perceiving that alone of all his treasure,
   Rest in the bottome lay.

For if I should (said he)
Bestow this jewell also on my creature,
He would adore my gifts in stead of me,
And rest in Nature, not the God of Nature.
   So both should losers be.

Yet let him keep the rest,
But keep them with repining restlessnesse:
Let him be rich and wearie, that at least,
If goodnesse leade him not, yet wearinesse
   May tosse him to my breast.

'The Pulley', by George Herbert

I have always liked this poem and it becomes more relevant as I get older.

SIR JOHN MILLS
ACTOR, PRODUCER AND DIRECTOR

Do not despair
For Johnny Head in Air,
He sleeps as sound
As Johnny underground.

Fetch out no shroud
For Johnny in the crowd,
But keep your tears
For him in after years.

Better by far
For Johnny the bright star,
To keep your head
And see his children fed.

'Johnny Head in Air', by John Pudney

I spoke this poem in a film called *The Way to the Stars*, which I made during the War. I have always admired it enormously as a piece of writing, as it is beautifully simple and makes a very true and accurate statement of the time.

ADRIAN MITCHELL
POET

I am Assistant to the Regional Commissioner
At Block E, Brooklands Avenue,
Communications Centre for Region 4,
Which used to be East Anglia.

I published several poems as a young man
But later found I could not meet my own high standards
So tore up all my poems and stopped writing.
(I stopped painting at eight and singing at five).
I was seconded to Block E
From the Ministry for the Environment.

Since there are no established poets available
I have come out here in my MPC,
(Maximum Protective Clothing),
To dictate some sort of poem or word-picture
Into a miniature cassette recorder.

When I first stepped out of Block E on to this beach
I could not record any words at all.
So I chewed two of the orange-flavoured pills
They give us for morale, switched on my Sony
And recorded this:

I am standing on the beach at Cambridge.
I can see a group in their MPC
Pushing Hoover-like and Ewbank-like machines
Through masses of black ashes.
The taller men are soldiers or police,
The others, scientific supervisors.
This group moves slowly across what seems
Like an endless car park with no cars at all.

I think that, in one moment,
All the books in Cambridge
Leapt off their shelves,
Spread their wings

And became white flames
And then black ash.
And I am standing on the beach at Cambridge.

You're a poet, said the Regional Commissioner,
Go out and describe that lot.

The University Library – a little hill of brick-dust.
King's College Chapel – a dune of stone-dust.
The sea is coming closer and closer.

The clouds are edged with green.
They are sagging low under some terrible weight.
They move more rapidly than usual.

Some younger women with important jobs
Were admitted to Block E
But my wife was a teacher in her forties.
We talked it over
When the nature of the crisis became apparent.
We agreed someone had to carry on.
That day I kissed her goodbye as I did every day
At the door of our house in Chesterton Road.
I kissed my son and my daughter goodbye.
I drove to Block E beside Hobson's Brook.
I felt like a piece of paper
Being torn in half.

And I am standing on the beach at Cambridge.
Some of the men in their MPC
Are sitting on the ground in the black ashes.
One is holding his head in both his hands.

I was forty-two three weeks ago.
My children painted me
Bright-coloured cards with poems for my birthday.
I stuck them with Blue-tack on the kitchen door.
I can remember the colours.

But in one moment all the children in Cambridge
Spread their wings
And became white flames
And then black ash.

And the children of America, I suppose.
And the children of Russia, I suppose.

And I am standing on the beach at Cambridge
And I am watching the broad black ocean tide
Bearing on its shoulders a burden of black ashes.

And I am listening to the last words of the sea
As it beats its head against the dying land.

'On the Beach at Cambridge', by Adrian Mitchell

The night is a dark blue balloon
The day is a golden balloon
The moon longs to cuddle the sun
The sun longs to cuddle the moon

'A Valentine Poem for Cathy Pope's kids at St Paul's
    Primary School, Cambridge', by Adrian Mitchell

I chose the longer piece because nothing is more important to me
than the fact that we are already embroiled in World War Three.
We must change, drastically, and begin to make peace. The shorter
piece I wrote for a group of six and seven-year-old children when
I realised that I was going to visit them on the day before Valentine's
Day. So I tried to remember what it was like to be in love at the
age of six or seven. The short poem is meant to be a spell to cleanse
the mind after the nightmare of the longer anti-poem. And to
celebrate the love of children, our only hope.

JESSICA MITFORD
WRITER

You may write me down in history
With your bitter, twisted lies,
You may trod me in the very dirt
But still, like dust, I'll rise.

Does my sassiness upset you?
Why are you beset with gloom?
'Cause I walk like I've got oil wells
Pumping in my living room.

Just like moons and like suns,
With the certainty of tides,
Just like hopes springing high,
Still I'll rise.

Did you want to see me broken?
Bowed head and lowered eyes?
Shoulders falling down like teardrops,
Weakened by my soulful cries.

Does my haughtiness offend you?
Don't you take it awful hard
'Cause I laugh like I've got gold mines
Diggin' in my own back yard.

You may shoot me with your words,
You may cut me with your eyes,
You may kill me with your hatefulness,
But still, like air, I'll rise.

Does my sexiness upset you?
Does it come as a surprise
That I dance like I've got diamonds
At the meeting of my thighs?

Out of the huts of history's shame
I rise
Up from a past that's rooted in pain
I rise
I'm a black ocean, leaping and wide,
Welling and swelling I bear in the tide.

Leaving behind nights of terror and fear
I rise
Into a daybreak that's wondrously clear
I rise
Bringing the gifts that my ancestors gave,
I am the dream and the hope of the slave.
I rise
I rise
I rise.

'Still I Rise', by Maya Angelou

Maya Angelou is a black writer whose works are immensely popular
in the United States but virtually unknown in England.

'And Still I Rise', from the volume of her poetry with the same
title, is in the great tradition of black American protest poetry. It
strikes me that in this period of racial strife, it may be particularly
important for the English reading public to absorb its message.

BEL MOONEY

WRITER AND BROADCASTER

In Aprell and in May,
When hartes be all mery,
Besse Bunting, the millaris may,
Withe lips so red as chery,
She cast in hir remembrance
To pass hir time in daliance
And to leve hir thought driery.
Right womanly arayd
In a peticote of whit,
She was nothing dismayd –
Hir countenance was full light.

'Besse Bunting', Anon.

This is an anonymous little poem from the early fifteenth century, which introduces us to Besse Bunting 'the miller's maid', who determines, one Spring morning, to 'pass her time in making love' and to leave her sad thoughts. That is all.

It is hard to explain why this poem delights me, because it is so simple, so lacking in obvious significance. So much poetry of the middle ages dwells upon God and death, as well it might, given the life expectancy of the time. Here though is the other side – the freshness and the love of life that you find most of all in the work of Chaucer. Spring is the key. About two hundred years earlier another anonymous poet wrote the famous 'Sumer is icumen in', with its vivid celebration of the teeming animal life and the growing seeds of Spring, and its exhortation to the cuckoo never to stop singing.

'Besse Bunting' has the same feeling – of joy after the long dark winter, of deer in the fields, of beauty. It celebrates one human being's decision not to be sad, but to go out and face the world, dressed in her best white skirt, and find what ever fun and 'daliance' she can. What an excellent idea! The poet says 'She was nothing dismayed', and his (or her?) admiration is clear: Besse is bold. No fear of death for her.

Poems like this speak warmly across the centuries. There are countless Besse Buntings today, all over the country, all fresh and keen and young, facing life happily and living for today. They could have giggled with this fifteenth century Besse. But who *was* the miller's daughter? We shall never know – but I am glad that her lips are forever red as cherries, on the page.

PATRICK MOORE
ASTRONOMER AND WRITER

War is a survival among us from savage times and affects now chiefly the boyish and unthinking element of the nation. The wisest realise that there are better ways for practicing heroism and other and more certain ends of insuring the survival of the fittest. It is something a people outgrow.

From: *Mars and its Canals*, by Percival Lowell

Professor Lowell, who believed Mars to be inhabited, wrote this nearly eighty years ago, but it is still true.

KENNETH MORGAN O.B.E.
DIRECTOR OF THE PRESS COUNCIL

Today we have naming of parts. Yesterday,
We had daily cleaning. And to-morrow morning,
We shall have what to do after firing. But to-day,
To-day we have naming of parts. Japonica
Glistens like coral in all of the neighbouring gardens
   And today we have naming of parts.

This is the lower sling swivel. And this
Is the upper sling swivel, whose use you will see
When you are given your slings. And this is the piling swivel,
Which in your case you have not got. The branches
Hold in the gardens their silent, eloquent gestures,
   Which in our case we have not got.

This is the safety-catch, which is always released
With an easy flick of the thumb. And please do not let me
See anyone using his finger. You can do it quite easy
If you have any strength in your thumb. The blossoms
Are fragile and motionless, never letting anyone see
   Any of them using their finger.

And this you can see is the bolt. The purpose of this
Is to open the breech, as you see. We can slide it
Rapidly backwards and forwards; we call this
Easing the spring. And rapidly backwards and forwards
The early bees are assaulting and fumbling the flowers:
   They call it easing the Spring.

They call it easing the Spring; it is perfectly easy
If you have any strength in your thumb: like the bolt,
And the breech, and the cocking-piece, and the point of
   balance,
Which in our case we have not got; and the almond-blossom
Silent in all of the gardens and the bees going backwards
   and forwards
   For today we have naming of parts.

'Naming of Parts', by Henry Reed

I chose 'Naming of Parts' for three reasons. The first is purely personal: I spent the gloriously warm cloudless summer of 1947 very happily as a soldier on Salisbury Plain. Mornings were usually devoted to drill and weapon training: afternoons, more leisurely, theoretically to map-reading but in practice to walking the Plain and downs above Tidworth reading poetry and plays and talking. No other piece of writing so sharply mirrors for me mornings passed in the ritual recitation of Army phrases and afternoons spent freely speculating on life, nature, language and art.

Its antiphonal voices make it appropriate to an anthology concerned with words and the delight they are for some and the problems they pose for others. One voice repeats them constantly, perhaps without knowing their quality and certainly unconscious of their poetry: the other, the responding sub-voice, has them whispering all the while in his head but cannot be speaking them aloud. There is fine irony in it.

Finally, read silently or aloud, it is probably one of the two best, and certainly one of the two most quoted, poems to have come out of the Second World War.

DESMOND MORRIS

ZOOLOGIST AND WRITER

The main conclusion arrived at in this work, namely that man is descended from some lowly organised form, will, I regret to think, be highly distasteful to many. But there can hardly be a doubt that we are descended from barbarians. The astonishment which I felt on first seeing a party of Fuegians on a wild and broken shore will never be forgotten by me, for the reflection at once rushed into my mind – such were our ancestors. These men were absolutely naked and bedaubed with paint, their long hair was tangled, their mouths frothed with excitement, and their expression was wild, startled, and distrustful. They possessed hardly any arts, and like wild animals lived on what they could catch; they had no government, and were merciless to every one not of their own small tribe. He who has seen a savage in his native land will not feel much shame, if forced to acknow-ledge that the blood of some more humble creature flows in his veins. For my own part I would as soon be descended from that heroic little monkey, who braved his dreaded enemy in order to save the life of his keeper, or from that old baboon, who descending from the mountains, carried away in triumph his young comrade from a crowd of astonished dogs – as from a savage who delights to torture his enemies, offers up bloody sacrifices, practises infanticide without remorse, treats his wives like slaves, knows no decency, and is haunted by the grossest superstitions.

Man may be excused for feeling some pride at having risen, though not through his own exertions, to the very summit of the organic scale; and the fact of his having thus risen, instead of having been aboriginally placed there, may give him hope for a still higher destiny in the distant future. But we are not here concerned with hopes or fears, only with the truth as far as our reason permits us to discover it; and I have given the evidence to the best of my ability. We must, however, acknowledge, as it seems to me, that man with all his noble qualities, with sympathy which feels for the most debased, with benevolence which extends not only to other men but to the humblest living creature, with his god-like intellect which has penetrated into the movements and constitution of the solar system – with all these exalted powers – Man still bears in his bodily frame the indelible stamp of his lowly origin.

From: *The Descent of Man*, by Charles Darwin

When I published *The Naked Ape* in 1967 I was attacked for stressing the 'beastliness' of man. I was told that to describe man as an animal was an assault on the dignity of the human race. To me, this revealed a singularly unhealthy attitude towards the other animals with which we share our planet. As a zoologist I had always marvelled at the wonderful complexity of animal life and I felt pride, not shame, at being a member of the animal kingdom. To see man as a risen ape rather than a fallen angel was for me the most heartening vision of our species. Yet there were those who were so outraged by my book that they had copies of it burned. There were moments when I felt that the clock had been turned back a hundred years, to the time when Charles Darwin was encountering similar reactions from Victorian society. Was his great message, his painstakingly assembled evidence of the truth of human evolution, still being misunderstood? I found this hard to believe, but clearly in certain quarters the blindess of rigid beliefs was still at loggerheads with the dogged honesty of Darwin's revelations.

So, in choosing a short piece of writing for this anthology I have turned, not to one of the many poems I have enjoyed, but to a passage from Darwin's book The Descent of Man, the final conclusion on the last two pages of that work. First published in 1871 it represents, along with his other volumes, the greatest single contribution to human thought since writing began, 5500 years ago.

JAN MORRIS
WRITER

A new voice hailed me of an old friend when, first returned from the Peninsula, I paced again in that long street of Damascus which is called Straight; and suddenly taking me wondering by the hand 'Tell me (said he), since thou art here again in the peace and assurance of Ullah, and whilst we walk, as in the former years, toward the new blossoming orchards, full of the sweet spring as the garden of God, what moved thee, or how couldst thou take such journeys into the fanatic Arabia?'

From: *Travels in Arabia Deserta*, by Charles Doughty

I have always loved the magnificent opening sentence of Charles Doughty's classic of 1888, partly for physical, partly for metaphysical reasons. Physical, because I find its rhythmic flow wonderfully sensual and exciting – years ago I set its opening words to music in my head, and I often sing them aloud when in a condition of particular elation. Metaphysical, because I think Doughty has written into the sentence suggestive undertones of symbolism and mysticism. Was there such a voice? Was there such a friend, to greet him home from Arabia out of the blue? I doubt it. The friend is that Other who is always somewhere about: the voice, the one we all hear sometimes, asking us why we do these things. And the street called Straight, whether in life or in art, leads us all (does it not?) towards the sweet spring of the garden of God.

JOHN MORTON
PSYCHOLINGUIST

The British Deep Fat Frying
Research Association

The following paragraphs are extracted from 'Fish and Chips, 1957,' the annual report of the British Deep Fat Frying Research Association.

1. Work on the six-story research establishment (to cost £1.25 millions) on an attractive site in the New Forest began in April, 1957. The Board of Research records with regret that by the end of the year the building was not ready for occupation.

2. When complete the new building will be equipped with six experimental fryers of an entirely new design. One of these will be large enough to hold 72 cwt. of chips at one charging and will be used in experiments to evolve methods of supplying chips to large formations of infantry (brigades or even divisions). Another of the fryers will be contained in a lead wall 4.7 ft. thick and will be used to make the first studies in this country of the influence of highly ionising radiations on the deep fat frying process. There will be a dining-floor and roof garden where teams of volunteers from Southampton and Eastbourne will be subjected to controlled feeding tests with fish and chips cooked in the experimental equipment.

3. In spite of a leak in its frying vessel which hampered experimental work for most of the summer, the Media Development Unit has made further progress in its classification of oils which can be used in deep fat frying. No fewer than 46 oils have been given placings in the Spode and Whetstone scales. Six mineral oils have been classified unsuitable for frying. Four were found to corrode equipment rapidly, one gave off toxic vapours that proved fatal to frying operatives not equipped with suitable masks, and one imparted an olive green colour to all organic materials (including human tissues) with which it came into contact.

4. Preliminary tests with an oil classified 45/S(7.3) have

shown that it offers a means of imparting a crisp brown texture to chips in as little as two seconds (at 830 deg. centigrade). It has indeed been possible to produce chips in which the entire potato body is converted into a hard brown material. Forty-five/S(7.3) is obtained by a process of dialytic concentration from the residues of holds of oil tankers plying to the Persian Gulf via the Cape. The oil, however, leaves a certain after-taste and fractional distillation techniques followed by absorption on resin exchange columns are being used in an attempt to isolate the principle which appears to give offence.

5. The Products Application Division has continued its studies of the properties of chips which have been subjected to deep freezing as a means of preservation. Earlier hopes that this process would offer a means of building up an export trade in fish and chips have not proved well founded. Deepfrozen chips have shown a tendency to mechanical failure during resuscitation. One consignment which was flown to New York and back in a chartered aircraft turned into a light blue granular powder when thawed out. The possibility that the powder may be of value as a thermal insulant for prefabricated buildings is being actively pursued.

6. During 1957 the Operational Research Division drew up specifications for an electronic computer, which should be delivered in 1958. Eventually it is intended to programme the machine for solving problems concerned with stocktaking and raw materials control in typical deep frying establishments. In the meantime it is expected that the machine will not be fully occupied on this work and that it will be possible to rent computing time to the Atomic Energy Authority.

7. The three vans of the Field Demonstration Unit have travelled widely throughout the country during 1957. The sale of surplus chips cooked in the vans during the year produced a gross income of £36,423.

8. The Board of Research feels that its report for 1957 cannot be concluded without a reference to the crippling shortage of skilled scientists and engineers in the deep fat frying industry. All the board's plans for research into the frying of fish as distinct from chips, have had to be postponed for yet another year, almost entirely because of the shortage

of men with postgraduate research degrees who can be attracted to work in the association's laboratories.

Our Scientific Correspondent regrets that the extracts are not fuller: he has, however, read the reports of many research associations lately.

JOHN MADDOX

From: *The Guardian*, 1 April 1958

Communication is essential to scientific progress. Too often, scientists are incapable of writing in a way that the layman can understand. This helps to maintain the mystique of science but is ultimately counter productive. The process is not helped by journalists who either fail to understand the ideas or who dramatize some minor aspect of a scientific work for the sake of a good headline. Here we have a first-rate example of good scientific journalism which shows what can be done. The date of the first appearance of this piece is not, perhaps, irrelevant.

ROBERT MULDOON

PRIME MINISTER OF NEW ZEALAND

For if the trumpet give an uncertain sound, who shall prepare himself to the battle? So likewise ye, except ye utter by the tongue words easy to be understood, how shall it be known what is spoken? For ye shall speak into the air.

1 *Corinthians*, XIV, verses 8 and 9.

I was brought up on a diet of the authorised version of the Bible and the sonorous ringing phrases in the archaic tongue will always have more substance for me than the quiet, precise modern versions which today's preachers always seem to ask me to use when I read the Lesson. Which has more impact, You are a skylark, not an ordinary bird, or Hail to thee blithe spirit, bird thou never wert? Could Shakespeare live with a modern version which said Friends, Romans, countrymen – listen to me, you lot? Could the 23rd Psalm ever be the same in modern English, even though the Presbyterians have mutilated it for generations?

Shortly after I entered Parliament, it became clear to me that I had too many friends. What I needed was some enemies. There was no way that I was ever going to get across the message that I wanted to give to the people of New Zealand if I used the soft, simple word, offending no-one and in fact being heard by no-one.

The message, as is the case with many new MPs, is contained in my maiden speech. It is a message of love for this country and its people, confidence in this country and its people, and a desire to preserve and enhance all that is good in our way of life for the benefit of future generations of New Zealanders.

Extract from: *My Way*, by Robert Muldoon

BRIAN PATTEN
POET

I

In a shoe-box stuffed in an old nylon stocking
Sleeps the baby mouse I found in the meadow,
Where he trembled and shook beneath a stick
Till I caught him up by the tail and brought him in,
Cradled in my hand,
A little quaker, the whole body of him trembling,
His absurd whiskers sticking out like a cartoon-mouse,
His feet like small leaves,
Little lizard-feet,
Whitish and spread wide when he tried to struggle away,
Wriggling like a minuscule puppy.

Now he's eaten his three kinds of cheese and drunk from his
    bottle-cap watering-trough –

So much he just lies in one corner,
His tail curled under him, his belly big
As his head; his bat-like ears
Twitching, tilting towards the least sound.

Do I imagine he no longer trembles
When I come close to him?
He seems no longer to tremble.

II

But this morning the shoe-box house on the back porch is
    empty.
Where has he gone, my meadow mouse,
My thumb of a child that nuzzled in my palm? –
To run under the hawk's wing,
Under the eye of the great owl watching from the elm-tree,
To live by courtesy of the shrike, the snake, the tom-cat.

I think of the nestling fallen into the deep grass,
The turtle gasping in the dusty rubble of the highway,

173

The paralytic stunned in the tub, and the water rising –
All things innocent, hapless, forsaken.

'The Meadow Mouse', by Theodore Roethke

I rescued a bee from a web last night.
It had been there several hours,
Numbed by the cold it could hardly fight
A spider half its size, one programmed
To string a web across the fattest flowers
And transform the pollen into bait.
My sympathy I know now was misplaced,
It had found the right time in which to die.
I saved it while light sank into grass
And trees swelled to claim their space;
I saved it in a time of surface peace.
Next morning as I watched the broken web gather light
Seeing it ruined in the grass I understood
That I had done more harm than good,
And I felt confused by that act
Of egocentric tenderness.
I called it love at first, then care,
Then simple curiosity,
But there was a starker reason for such sympathy.
It is that one day I too will be caught out in the cold,
And finding terror in there being no help at hand
Will invent a God who
Will remember how once I tried to save a bee ...
Though I hope the same mess is not made of me.

'One Reason for Sympathy', from *Grave Gossip*, by Brian
Patten

To my knowledge there are not many creatures that will go out of their way to help another species, and it baffles me that the one most likely to – Man – is also the cruellest. I've chosen 'The Meadow Mouse' because it made me think about the above, and have included a poem of my own because in it I've tried to provide one reason –a not very gracious one – as to why we do help other creatures.

SIR PETER PEARS
SINGER

Extract from the *Nonsense Gazette*, for August, 1870.

Our readers will be interested in the following communications from our valued and learned contributor, Professor Bosh, whose labours in the fields of Culinary and Botanical science, are so well known to all the world. The first three Articles richly merit to be added to the Domestic cookery of every family; those which follow, claim the attention of all Botanists, and we are happy to be able through Dr Bosh's kindness to present our readers with illustrations of his discoveries. All the new flowers are found in the valley of Verrikwier, near the lake of Oddgrow, and on the summit of the hill Orfeltugg.

THREE RECEIPTS FOR DOMESTIC COOKERY

TO MAKE AN AMBLONGUS PIE

Take 4 pounds (say 4½ pounds) of fresh Amblongusses, and put them in a small pipkin.

Cover them with water and boil them for 8 hours incessantly, after which add 2 pints of new milk, and proceed to boil for 4 hours more.

When you have ascertained that the Amblongusses are quite soft, take them out and place them in a wide pan, taking care to shake them well previously.

Grate some nutmeg over the surface, and cover them carefully with powdered gingerbread, curry-powder, and a sufficient quantity of Cayenne papper.

Remove the pan into the next room, and place it on the floor. Bring it back again, and let it simmer for three-quarters of an hour.

Shake the pan violently till all the Amblongusses have become of a pale purple colour.

Then, having prepared the paste, insert the whole carefully, adding at the same time a small pigeon, 2 slices of beef, 4 cauliflowers, and any number of oysters.

Watch patiently till the crust begins to rise, and add a pinch of salt from time to time.

Serve up in a clean dish, and throw the whole out of window as fast as possible.

TO MAKE CRUMBOBBLIOUS CUTLETS

Procure some strips of beef, and having cut them into the smallest possible slices, proceed to cut them still smaller, eight or perhaps nine times.

When the whole is thus minced, brush it up hastily with a new clothes-brush, and stir round rapidly and capriciously with a salt-spoon or a soup-ladle.

Place the whole in a saucepan, and remove it to a sunny place, – say the roof of the house if free from sparrows or other birds, – and leave it there for about a week.

At the end of that time add a little lavender, some oil of almonds, and a few herring-bones; and then cover the whole with 4 gallons of clarified crumbobblious sauce, when it will be ready for use.

Cut it into the shape of ordinary cutlets, and serve up in a clean tablecloth or dinner-napkin.

TO MAKE GOSKY PATTIES

Take a Pig, three or four years of age, and tie him by the off-hind leg to a post. Place 5 pounds of currants, 3 of sugar, 2 pecks of peas, 18 roast chestnuts, a candle, and six bushels of turnips, within his reach; if he eats these, constantly provide him with more.

Then procure some cream, some slices of Cheshire cheese, four quires of foolscap paper, and a packet of black pins. Work the whole into a paste, and spread it out to dry on a sheet of clean brown waterproof linen.

When the paste is perfectly dry, but not before, proceed to beat the Pig violently, with the handle of a large broom. If he squeals, beat him again.

Visit the paste and beat the Pig alternately for some days, and ascertain if at the end of that period the whole is about to turn into Gosky Patties.

If it does not then, it never will; and in that case the Pig may be let loose, and the whole process may be considered as finished.

'Nonsense Cookery', by Edward Lear

Humour and with it nonsense are desirable and delightful elements of life. Edward Lear is best known to the majority of people for his Limericks which, illustrated by himself, have delighted people for a hundred years and more. He was also of course a fine topographical artist, and a painter of birds and landscapes. He suffered from illness (petit mal) all his life and was very conscious of his own 'homeliness'. Here is a charming little poem about him by W. H. Auden:

EDWARD LEAR

Left by his friend to breakfast alone on the white
Italian shore, his Terrible Demon arose
Over his shoulder; he wept to himself in the night,
A dirty landscape-painter who hated his nose.

The legions of cruel inquisitive They
Were so many and big like dogs: he was upset
By Germans and boats; affection was miles away:
But guided by tears he successfully reached his Regret.

How prodigious the welcome was. Flowers took his hat
And bore him off to introduce him to the tongs;
The demon's false nose made the table laugh; a cat
Soon had him waltzing madly, let him squeeze her hand;
Words pushed him to the piano to sing comic songs;
And children swarmed to him like settlers. He became a
    land.

W. H. Auden (1939)

DR MAX PERUTZ
MOLECULAR BIOLOGIST

To the London *Nation* for August 15, 1914

Sir

Against the vast majority of my countrymen, even at this moment, in the name of humanity and civilization, I protest against our share in the destruction of Germany.

A month ago Europe was a peaceful comity of nations; if an Englishman killed a German, he was hanged. Now, if an Englishman kills a German, or if a German kills an Englishman, he is a patriot, who has deserved well of his country. We scan the newspapers with greedy eyes for news of slaughter, and rejoice when we read of innocent young men, blindly obedient to the word of command, mown down in thousands by the machine-guns of Liège. Those who saw the London crowds, during the nights leading up to the Declaration of War saw a whole population, hitherto peaceable and humane, precipitated in a few days down the steep slope to primitive barbarism, letting loose, in a moment, the instincts of hatred and blood lust against which the whole fabric of society has been raised. 'Patriots' in all countries acclaim this brutal orgy as a noble determination to vindicate the right; reason and mercy are swept away in one great flood of hatred; dim abstractions of unimaginable wickedness – Germany to us and the French, Russia to the Germans – conceal the simple fact that the enemy are men, like ourselves, neither better nor worse – men who love their homes and the sunshine, and all the simple pleasures of common lives; men now mad with terror in the thought of their wives, their sisters, their children, exposed, with our help, to the tender mercies of the conquering Cossack.

And all this madness, all this rage, all this flaming death of our civilization and our hopes, has been brought about because a set of official gentlemen, living luxurious lives, mostly stupid, and all without imagination or heart, have chosen that it should occur rather than that any one of them should suffer some infinitesimal rebuff to his country's pride.

No literary tragedy can approach the futile horror of the White Paper. The diplomatists, seeing from the first the inevitable end, mostly wishing to avoid it, yet drifted from hour to hour of the swift crisis, restrained by punctilio from making or accepting the small concessions that might have saved the world, hurried on at last by blind fear to loose the armies for the work of mutual butchery.

And behind the diplomatists, dimly heard in the official documents, stand vast forces of national greed and national hatred – atavistic instincts, harmful to mankind at its present level, but transmitted from savage and half-animal ancestors, concentrated and directed by Governments and the Press, fostered by the upper class as a distraction from social discontent, artificially nourished by the sinister influence of the makers of armaments, encouraged by a whole foul literature of 'glory', and by every text-book of history with which the minds of children are polluted.

England, no more than other nations which participate in this war, can be absolved either as regards its national passions or as regards its diplomacy.

For the past ten years, under the fostering care of the Government and a portion of the Press, a hatred of Germany has been cultivated and a fear of the German Navy. I do not suggest that Germany has been guiltless; I do not deny that the crimes of Germany have been greater than our own. But I do say that whatever defensive measures were necessary should have been taken in a spirit of calm foresight, not in a wholly needless turmoil of panic and suspicion. It is this deliberately created panic and suspicion that produced the public opinion by which our participation in the war has been rendered possible.

Our diplomacy, also, has not been guiltless. Secret arrangements, concealed from Parliament and even (at first) from almost all the Cabinet, created, in spite of reiterated denials, an obligation suddenly revealed when the war fever had reached the point which rendered public opinion tolerant of the discovery that the lives of many, and the livelihood of all, had been pledged by one man's irresponsible decisions. Yet, though France knew our obligations, Sir E. Grey refused, down to the last moment, to inform Germany of the conditions of our neutrality or of our intervention. On

August 1st he reports as follows a conversation with the German Ambassador (No. 123):

'He asked me whether, if Germany gave a promise not to violate Belgian neutrality, we would engage to remain neutral. I replied that I could not say that; our hands were still free, and we were considering what our attitude should be. All I could say was that our attitude would be determined largely by public opinion here, and that the neutrality of Belgium would appeal very strongly to public opinion here. I did not think that we could give a promise of neutrality on that condition alone. The Ambassador pressed me as to whether I could not formulate conditions on which we would remain neutral. He even suggested that the integrity of France and her colonies might be guaranteed. I said I felt obliged to refuse definitely any promise to remain neutral on similar terms, and I could only say that we must keep our hands free.'

It thus appears that the neutrality of Belgium, the integrity of France and her colonies, and the naval defence of the northern and western coasts of France, were all mere pretexts. If Germany had agreed to our demands in all these respects, we should still not have promised neutrality.

I cannot resist the conclusion that the Government has failed in its duty to the nation by not revealing long-standing arrangements with the French, until, at the last moment, it made them the basis of an appeal to honour; that it has failed in its duty to Europe by not declaring its attitude at the beginning of the crisis; and that it has failed in its duty to humanity by not informing Germany of conditions which would insure its non-participation in a war which, whatever its outcome, must cause untold hardship and the loss of many thousands of our bravest and noblest citizens.

Yours, etc.
Bertrand Russell

August 12, 1914

From: *Autobiography*, by Bertrand Russell

My favourite passage is a letter to *The Nation* (forerunner of the present *New Statesman*), written by the great philosopher Bertrand Russell shortly after the outbreak of the First World War. It testifies to a remarkable independence of mind, penetrating judgment and moral courage. As grandson of a prime minister Russell had grown up among the elite, which left him with no respect for rank without brains or integrity. He had the clear-headed vision to see through patriotic rhetoric. When politicians and churchmen were stoking the flames of hatred, Russell, an atheist from adolescence, upheld true Christian values. It takes immense strength of mind to dissociate oneself from the passionate views of all around one and regard a situation coolly from outside. Russell's pacifist campaign earned him the hatred of the public (he was nearly lynched on one occasion), expulsion from Trinity College and imprisonment, but history has proved him right. Europe would not have fallen to totalitarianism if the slaughter had been stopped. Russell's letter inspired me during the Falklands Crisis when I felt that no-one should be killed over an issue that could be settled peacefully, seeing that sovereignty over the Falklands will sooner or later have to be handed over to the Argentine whatever the outcome of the war.

GERALD PRIESTLAND
WRITER AND BROADCASTER

Again the modern era has undoubtedly given new opportunities for dishonesty in trade. The advance of knowledge has discovered new ways of making things appear other than they are, and has rendered possible many new forms of adulteration. The producer is now far removed from the ultimate consumer; and his wrong doings are not visited with the prompt and sharp punishment which falls on the head of a person who, being bound to live and die in his native village, plays a dishonest trick on one of his neighbours. The opportunities for knavery are certainly more numerous than they were; but there is no reason for thinking that people avail themselves of a larger proportion of such opportunities than they used to do. On the contrary, modern methods of trade imply habits of trustfulness on the one side and a power of resisting temptation to dishonesty on the other, which do not exist among a backward people. Instances of simple truth and personal fidelity are met with under all social conditions: but those who have tried to establish a business of modern type in a backward country find that they can scarcely ever depend on the native population for filling posts of trust. It is even more difficult to dispense with imported assistance for work which calls for a strong moral character than for that which requires great skill and mental ability.

There are thus strong reasons for doubting whether the moral character of business in the modern age compares as unfavourably as is sometimes supposed with that of earlier times. At all events, while the controversy on this point is still unsettled, it is best to describe that character by a term that does not imply any moral qualities, whether good or evil, but which indicates the undisputed fact that modern business is characterised by more self-reliant habits, more forethought, more deliberate and free choice. There is not any one term adequate for this purpose: but FREEDOM OF INDUSTRY AND ENTERPRISE, or more shortly, ECONOMIC

FREEDOM, points in the right direction, and may be used in the absence of a better.

From: *Principles of Economics*, by Alfred Marshall (second edition, 1891)

I must admit that, for me, part of the appeal of this great work – the Old Testament of Economics during my PPE days at Oxford – lies in its shocking unfashionableness: in its patronising references to backward countries, knavery, and natives incapable of holding positions of trust. Here speaks Victorian Imperialism in the full flight of self-confidence, untrammelled by any twinges of guilt or cultural relativity. What is good for Manchester must also be good for the citizens of Bombay, if only they were advanced enough to see it. And it dawns upon you that people like Marshall were not bloodthirsty exploiters (or did not see themselves as such) but men who believed in absolute and immutable standards. They were also writers of majestic prose, the likes of which is not penned today. It exudes authority and confidence, not only political but literary. Firmly rooted in classical education and the cadences of Cicero, Marshall erects his enormous sentences with architectural grace and style, yet without ever losing sight of his meaningful purpose. He achieves clarity without crude simplicity. Try reading the passage out loud and you will emerge invigorated: for behind it all lies a powerful sense of rhythm, a rhythm developed by Marshall's innate sense of oratory, one of the gifts of the ancient Roman ruler. This is ruling class prose, perhaps no longer appropriate to our times, for the fact is nobody has the confidence or authority to write it today.

MARJORIE PROOPS O.B.E.

JOURNALIST

Let me not to the marriage of true minds
Admit impediments. Love is not love
Which alters when it alteration finds,
Or bends with the remover to remove:
O, no! it is an ever-fixed mark,
That looks on tempests, and is never shaken;
It is the star to every wandering bark,
Whose worth's unknown, although his height be taken.
Love's not Time's fool, though rosy lips and cheeks
Within his bending sickle's compass come;
Love alters not with his brief hours and weeks,
But bears it out even to the edge of doom.
    If this be error, and upon me proved,
    I never writ, nor no man ever loved.

Sonnet 116, by William Shakespeare

I grew up reading sauce bottle labels, Damon Runyon, Jane Austen, the Bible (preferring the rude bits) and Shakespeare's sonnets.

Not the plays. They were school WORK. The sonnets were for pleasure; for their mystery and tenderness and for their intense romance.

And although I can quote snatches from HP labels, and bits from the Book of Ruth, I can drive friends potty reciting sonnets. 'Let me not . . .' is my number one. It is the most moving definition of love that I know. I chose it because love is the tool and the very basis of my trade.

MAGNUS PYKE
SCIENTIST, WRITER AND BROADCASTER

O world invisible, we view thee,
O world intangible, we touch thee,
O world unknowable, we know thee,
Inapprehensible, we clutch thee!

Does the fish soar to find the ocean,
The eagle plunge to find the air –
That we ask of the stars in motion
If they have rumour of thee there?

Not where the wheeling systems darken,
And our benumbed conceiving soars! –
The drift of pinions, would we harken,
Beats at our own clay-shuttered doors.

The angels keep their ancient places; –
Turn but a stone and start a wing!
'Tis ye, 'tis your estranged faces,
That miss the many-splendoured thing.

But (when so sad thou canst not sadder)
Cry; – and upon thy so sore loss
Shall shine the traffic of Jacob's ladder
Pitched between Heaven and Charing Cross.

Yea, in the night, my Soul, my daughter,
Cry, – clinging Heaven by the hems;
And lo, Christ walking on the water
Not of Gennesareth, but Thames!

'In No Strange Land', by Francis Thompson

This poem does not need much comment from me. I chose it
because it describes the very nature of science by which we are
discovering what kind of universe we are living in and how wisely
to adapt it to our service.

RANDOLPH QUIRK

VICE-CHANCELLOR, UNIVERSITY OF LONDON

Now as I was young and easy under the apple boughs
About the lilting house and happy as the grass was green,
   The night above the dingle starry,
     Time let me hail and climb
    Golden in the heydays of his eyes,
And honoured among wagons I was prince of the apple
       towns
And once below a time I lordly had the trees and leaves
    Trail with daisies and barley
   Down the rivers of the windfall light.

And as I was green and carefree, famous among the barns
About the happy yard and singing as the farm was home,
   In the sun that is young once only,
     Time let me play and be
    Golden in the mercy of his means,
And green and golden I was huntsman and herdsman, the
       calves
Sang to my horn, the foxes on the hills barked clear and
       cold,
    And the sabbath rang slowly
   In the pebbles of the holy streams.

All the sun long it was running, it was lovely, the hay
Fields high as the house, the tunes from the chimneys, it
      was air
   And playing, lovely and watery
     And fire green as grass.
    And nightly under the simple stars
As I rode to sleep the owls were bearing the farm away,
All the moon long I heard, blessed among stables, the night-
      jars
   Flying with the ricks, and the horses
    Flashing into the dark.

And then to awake, and the farm, like a wanderer white
With the dew, come back, the cock on his shoulder: it was
        all
    Shining, it was Adam and maiden,
        The sky gathered again
    And the sun grew round that very day
So it must have been after the birth of the simple light
In the first, spinning place, the spellbound horses walking
        warm
    Out of the whinnying green stable
        On to the fields of praise.

And honoured among foxes and pheasants by the gay house
Under the new made clouds and happy as the heart was
        long,
    In the sun born over and over,
        I ran my heedless ways,
    My wishes raced through the house high hay
And nothing I cared, at my sky blue trades, that time allows
In all his tuneful turning so few and such morning songs
    Before the children green and golden
        Follow him out of grace,

Nothing I cared, in the lamb white days, that time would
        take me
Up to the swallow thronged loft by the shadow of my hand,
    In the moon that is always rising.
        Nor that riding to sleep
    I should hear him fly with the high fields
And wake to the farm forever fled from the childless land.
Oh as I was young and easy in the mercy of his means,
    Time held me green and dying
    Though I sang in my chains like the sea.

'Fern Hill', by Dylan Thomas

Searching through the pages of lost time gives a compelling
bitter-sweet nostalgia that few of us can resist. Looking back on
our childhood is especially evocative – and it is worth remembering
that the word *nostalgia* is from Greek elements meaning 'the pain

of returning home'. Sometimes we may suspect that we are sentimentally exaggerating past magic and we may overreact by deliberately minimising it, as Philip Larkin does in his ironical 'I remember, I remember'. But we are still crying out with 'home-pain' nonetheless.

As Wordsworth puts it in the well-known Immortality Ode which Dylan Thomas obviously had in his mind, 'Heaven lies about us in our infancy'. But Thomas's poem, while deeply religious in its sense of the holy and in its echoes of Genesis, is especially preoccupied with the magic of a child's creative imagination, 'green and golden'. And Thomas's own creative imagination, as well as his sheer lust for the lusciousness of language, enables us to recreate for ourselves the fast-running make-believe, the lordly roles and the mystical powers we did not dare to tell even an indulgent mother and now would be too shy, too staid, too muted by the grimness of adult reality, to put into words ourselves.

I have no doubt that the poem rouses the images of childhood for everyone, but as a farmer's son I find it redolent of images and memories that seem uniquely my own. I know what it meant for hayfields to be 'high as the house', for calves to 'sing to my horn' as huntsman. I know what it meant to awake, and to find the farm, 'like a wanderer white with the dew, come back'. And I know what it means when now I 'wake to the farm forever fled from the childless land'.

JOHN RAE
HEADMASTER OF WESTMINSTER SCHOOL

We have not realised religion in its perfection, even as we have not realised God. Religion of our conception, being thus imperfect, is always subject to a process of evolution. And if all faiths outlined by men are imperfect, the question of comparative merit does not arise.

Even as a tree has a single trunk, but many branches and leaves, so there is one true and perfect Religion, but it becomes many, as it passes through the human medium. The one Religion is beyond all speech. Imperfect men put it into such language as they can command, and their words are interpreted by other men equally imperfect. Whose interpretation is to be held to be the right one? Everybody is right from his own standpoint, but it is not possible that everybody is wrong. Hence the necessity of tolerance, which does not mean indifference to one's own faith, but a more intelligent and purer love for it. Tolerance gives us spiritual insight, which is as far from fanaticism as the North Pole from the South. True knowledge of religion breaks down the barriers between faith and faith.

From: *All Men are Brothers – The Life and Thoughts of Mahatma Gandhi*

This superb passage from the writing of Mahatma Gandhi expresses the openness to and tolerance of other religions that I believe the world needs. Religious intolerance, religious bigotry and religious exclusiveness are still with us though we might have thought that they had disappeared hundreds of years ago. Gandhi's simple yet profound insight into the nature of true religion says all that matters about the basis of tolerance. Above all it emphasises that tolerance is not just another word for indifference.

I first read this passage ten years ago; it was like finding a signpost after years of searching for the right direction in a religious jungle. It still seems to me the most sane and humane statement on religion that I have read. Perhaps that was why Gandhi was assassinated by a religious fanatic.

ESTHER RANTZEN
BROADCASTER AND PRODUCER/PRESENTER OF 'THAT'S LIFE'

There was a time when meadow, grove and stream
The earth, and every common sight,
To me did seem
Apparelled in celestial light,
The glory and the freshness of a dream.
It is not now as it hath been of yore: –
Turn wheresoe'er I may,
By night or day,
The things which I have seen I now can see no more.

The rainbow comes and goes,
And lovely is the Rose
The Moon doth with delight
Look round her when the heavens are bare,
Waters on a starry night
Are beautiful and fair;
The sunshine is a glorious birth;
But yet I know, where'er I go,
That there hath past away a glory from the earth ...

– But there's a Tree, of many, one,
A single Field which I have looked upon,
Both of them speak of something that is gone;
The pansy at my feet
Doth the same tale repeat:
Whither is fled the visionary gleam?
Where is it now, the glory and the dream?

Our birth is but a sleep and a forgetting:
The Soul that rises with us, our life's Star,
Hath had elsewhere its setting
And cometh from afar:
Not in entire forgetfulness,
And not in utter nakedness,
But trailing clouds of glory do we come
From God, who is our home:

Heaven lies about us in our infancy!
Shades of the prison-house begin to close
Upon the growing boy,
But he beholds the light, and whence it flows,
He sees it in his joy;
The Youth, who daily farther from the east
Must travel, still is Nature's Priest,
And by the vision splendid
Is on his way attended;
At length the Man perceives it die away,
And fade into the light of common day.

From: 'Ode on the Intimations of Immortality from
Recollections of Early Childhood', by William Wordsworth

I remember first reading this poem at school, and thinking that
Wordsworth couldn't possibly have invented it – some of the lines
are so perfect they seem always to have existed – he must just
have uncovered them, like a diamond under the earth. 'Our birth
is but a sleep and a forgetting' is an idea that has stayed with
me all my life – The idea that all children have a bright vision
that slowly fades 'into the light of common day' has become even
truer for me, now I have children of my own. And for people
who, like me, spend their whole lives, reluctantly, in big cities,
this poem creates a memory of the Maytime countryside, that
Londoners can only dream about.

FREDERIC RAPHAEL
WRITER

What are we waiting for, assembled in the forum?

    The barbarians are due here today.

Why isn't anything going on in the senate?
Why are the senators sitting there without legislating?

    Because the barbarians are coming today.
    What's the point of senators making laws now?
    Once the barbarians are here, they'll do the legislating.

Why did our emperor get up so early,
and why is he sitting enthroned at the city's main gate,
in state, wearing the crown?

    Because the barbarians are coming today
    and the emperor's waiting to receive their leader.
    He's even got a scroll to give him,
    loaded with titles, with imposing names.

Why have our two consuls and praetors come out today
wearing their embroidered, their scarlet togas?
Why have they put on bracelets with so many amethysts,
rings sparkling with magnificent emeralds?
Why are they carrying elegant canes
beautifully worked in silver and gold?

    Because the barbarians are coming today
    and things like that dazzle the barbarians.

Why don't our distinguished orators turn up as usual
to make their speeches, say what they have to say?

    Because the barbarians are coming today
    and they're bored by rhetoric and public speaking.

Why this sudden bewilderment, this confusion?
(How serious people's faces have become.)
Why are the streets and squares emptying so rapidly,
everyone going home lost in thought?

  Because night has fallen and the barbarians haven't come.
  And some of our men just in from the border say
  there are no barbarians any longer.

Now what's going to happen to us without barbarians?
Those people were a kind of solution.

'Waiting for the Barbarians', by C. P. Cavafy (translated
        by Edmund Keeley and Philip Sherrard)

Though more passionately and typically Greek than any other poet
of that undying tradition, Cavafy was not a native of mainland
Greece and rarely visited it. But to be a Greek is not a matter
of inhabiting that small and rumpled country that the atlas labels
Greece. The word 'atlas', after all, is one which embraces the whole
globe, just as the giant Atlas, in the myth, was supposed to sustain
the heavens on his shoulders; we use a Greek term to speak of
a volume in which every country is mapped. Greekness is a state
of mind as well as a matter of strict nationality. What is a Greek
but a man who feels himself to be so? Only last week, in an elevator
in Los Angeles, I heard Greek spoken, greeted the speakers in
my own halting demotic and was promptly involved in an exchange
of passwords, amongst which figured, of course, the name of
Cavafy.

In 1962, we went to Greece for the first time. I discovered that
the modern language, always said to be so different from the
ancient, was much more accessible than I dared to hope. The more
common words, like those for bread and water, were not familiar
to me, but many of the longer ones were: a soldier was still
stratiotis, just as he was in Thucydides, and a blacksmith still went
under the name of the armourer of the Gods, Hephaestos. Myth
lives close under the language, just as the rocky skeleton of Hellas
does below the modern concrete surface.

Cavafy is a miniaturist, true to an Alexandrian tradition which
goes back at least to Callimachus. He is Alexandrian also in his
allusiveness and in his eclecticism. His eroticism is Pagan, but
he could hardly be as hellenic as he was and not acknowledge

the pervasive authority of the Greek church, the means by which Greek culture was able to survive during long years of humiliation by conquerors of all kinds. It is a mystery to me that a homosexual poet, obsessed with the eroticism of his youth, and of its missed opportunities, can speak with such a universal voice. He turned his personal history and that of a small and, so they say, not particularly impressive city into an art of meticulous refinement and singularly general application. Even now I cannot promise to read his work without a crib, but I turn to it frequently and not a day now passes without my attempting to make out the meaning of at least one page of Ritsos, Sepheris or Cavafy.

Cavafy's output was quite small and his work can be encompassed almost at a single reading; he recruits one so rapidly to his world that, reading for the first time of a young man called Raphael, a denizen of the vanished culture which the poet so silkily resuscitates, one has a sense of belonging to the citizenship of Alexandria as it once was, polymorphous as the old man of the sea himself. Now the cross-fertilising cultures of the Mediterranean have been winnowed into apparently irreconcilable factions. I cannot wholly salute the narrow enthusiasms that have been the consequence of Ottoman decline and western intrusion; I have chosen Cavafy's 'The Barbarians Are Coming' with the sinking feeling of one who fears that, God help us, they are already here.

SEELEY: ... What about that game on Saturday, eh?

KEDGE: You were going to tell me. You haven't told me yet.

BARMAN: What game? Fulham?

SEELEY: No, the firm. Firm's got a team, see? Play on Saturdays.

BARMAN: Who d'you ... you play?

SEELEY: Other firms.

BARMAN: You boys in the team, are you?

KEDGE: Yes, I've been off sick though. I didn't play last week.

BARMAN: Sick, eh? You want to try one of my sausages, don't he, Henry?

OLD MAN: Oh, ay, yes.

KEDGE: What happened with the game, then?
   They move to the bench.

SEELEY: Well, when you couldn't play, Gidney moved Albert to left back.

KEDGE: He's a left half.

SEELEY: I know he's a left half. I said to Gidney myself, I said to him, look, why don't you go left back, Gidney? He said, no, I'm too valuable at centre half.

KEDGE: He didn't, did he?

SEELEY: Yes. Well, you know who was on the right wing, don't you? Connor.

KEDGE: Who? Tony Connor?

SEELEY: No. You know Connor. What's the matter with you? You've played against Connor

KEDGE: Oh – whatsisname – Micky Connor.

SEELEY: Yes.

KEDGE: I thought he'd given up the game.

SEELEY: No, what are you talking about? He plays for the printing works, plays outside right for the printing works.

KEDGE: He's a good ballplayer, that Connor, isn't he?

SEELEY: Look. I said to Albert before the kick off, Connor's on the right wing, I said, play your normal game. I told him six times before the kick off.

KEDGE: What's the good of him playing his normal game? He's a left half, he's not a left back.

SEELEY: Yes, but he's a defensive left half, isn't he? That's why I told him to play his normal game. You don't want to worry about Connor, I said, he's a good ballplayer but he's not all that good.

KEDGE: Oh, he's good, though.

SEELEY: No one's denying he's good. But he's not all that good. I mean, he's not tip-top. You know what I mean?

KEDGE: He's fast.

SEELEY: He's fast, but he's not all that fast, is he?

KEDGE: (*doubtfully*): Well, not all that fast ...

SEELEY: What about Levy? Was Levy fast?

KEDGE: Well, Levy was a sprinter.

SEELEY: He was a dasher, Levy. All he knew was run.

KEDGE: He could move.

SEELEY: Yes, but look how Albert played him! He cut him off, he played him out of the game. And Levy's faster than Connor.

KEDGE: Yes, but he wasn't so clever, though.

SEELEY: Well, what about Foxall?

KEDGE: Who? Lou Foxall?

SEELEY: No, you're talking about Lou Fox, I'm talking about Sandy Foxall.

KEDGE: Oh, the winger.

SEELEY: Sure. He was a very smart ballplayer, Foxall. But what did Albert do? He played his normal game. He let him come. He waited for him. And Connor's not as clever as Foxall.

KEDGE: He's clever though.

SEELEY: Gawd blimey, I know he's clever, but he's not as clever as Foxall, is he?

KEDGE: The trouble is, with Connor, he's fast too, isn't he?

SEELEY: But if Albert would have played his normal game! He played a game foreign to him.

KEDGE: How many'd Connor get?

SEELEY: He made three and scored two.

Pause. They eat.

KEDGE: No wonder he's depressed, Old Albert.

SEELEY: Oh, he was very depressed after the game, I can tell you. And of course Gidney was after him, of course. You know Gidney.

KEDGE: That berk.

(*Pause.*)

OLD MAN: Yes, he was sitting over where you are now, wasn't he, Fred? Looking very compressed with himself. Light-haired bloke, ain't he?

SEELEY: Yes, light-haired.

From: *A Night Out*, by Harold Pinter

Asked to choose '... a piece of writing you particularly enjoy' I have gone for just that – enjoyment.

The conversation from Harold Pinter's play offers a variety of pleasures. There is the pleasure of recognition – the seemingly familiar which confirms expectations at the same time as it surprises. There is the pleasure of style – hearing the unmistakable music of the author through the voices of his characters. And there is the inexhaustible pleasure of the subject itself – football.

BRIAN RIX C.B.E.

SECRETARY GENERAL OF THE ROYAL SOCIETY FOR MENTALLY
HANDICAPPED CHILDREN AND ADULTS (M.E.N.C.A.P.)

I was still working in the mat shop and in 1941 Mr Treece got two new boys from the female side. The boys were Ernie and Victor. Mr Treece asked Ernie to help me sort out the wool. When I wanted something or to tell him something I made some noises to make him understand. It was not easy at first but Ernie did not give in. He tried very hard until he began to understand me. Six months later Arthur was taken to Male Ward A1 because he had bronchitis. I was with Harold Sparks but he took a long time to understand me. My aunt and Grandma came to see me in February 1942. When Ernie was transferred to the male side and came in to me I tried to say hello to him. I tried three times before he understood. Then he said 'Hello, Joey'. I told Ernie that Arthur had gone to Male Ward A1 with bronchitis. The Sunday that followed Ernie's arrival, my cousin Ann and her friend came to see me. Harold also had a visit that day. I wanted to talk to my cousin Annie but it was very difficult; Arthur was in A1, Harold had a visit. There was nobody who could understand me. I made signs and pointed to Ernie. Mr Harris understood me and brought Ernie and I introduced him to my cousin. He understood me. That's how it all began. This was the first time I started to talk a little. We asked her how she liked the ATS. I was 22 at that time. My cousin was very pleased that she could understand me. Ernie was very good. When she went home she told Grandma how she was able to speak to me through Ernie. In May my brother returned from the army. He came to see me. I called Ernie who crawled on the floor and Peter picked him up and sat him on the chair. I introduced them to each other and Ernie repeated to Peter everything I said. Peter did not believe anybody could understand me.

From: *Tongue Tied*, by Joseph John Deacon

The story of Joseph John Deacon is now well-known around the world. His book *Tongue Tied* and the subsequent television production 'Joey' have brought a fame which is possibly more justified than most.

Unable, because of his handicap, to make himself understood by those around him, he lived in a silent world until the arrival of a young boy, Ernie Roberts who, understanding his painful attempts at speech, interpreted his needs.

Later the two friends, Joey and Ernie, both severely handicapped, were joined by two other mentally handicapped men, Tom and Michael, who had no physical disability. Michael was the only one of the four able to write a few sentences, but Tom, who could neither read nor write, taught himself to type by means of a code.

This extract gives some idea of the wondrous transition. I'm delighted to offer it as illustrating an understanding of words beyond our ken. I am proud that the Royal Society for Mentally Handicapped Children and Adults first published this book in 1974 and that Joey was able to taste the fruits of its success, by living in a house with his friends, until his death in 1981. The royalties made much possible. As the *Sunday Times* wrote: 'This book is a miracle'.

ROBERT ROBINSON
WRITER AND BROADCASTER

Somewhere in the South Atlantic, off the charted ship lanes, there is thought to be a vast turgid eddy known as the Sargasso Sea in which the derelicts of the seven seas ultimately come to rest. (My authority for the foregoing is a noted oceanographer named Turgid Eddie whom I met in a small West Side laboratory a few days ago and who drank nothing but Scotch and sea water.) Now this theory is all very well for schoolgirls and neurotic women, but the actual Sargasso is nowhere near the South Atlantic. It is situated in half a quarter section of rolling scrub midway between New York and Philadelphia, and embodies the worst features of both. At its core stands the shabby-genteel spokesman of these lines, slowly shedding his sanity as a terrifying vortex of dogs, debts and petty afflictions swirls sluggishly about his knees.

I might have dragged out my days in our gravel pit in peace, a myopic bookworm in sleeve garters and an alpaca jacket content to fuss among his ageratum, but for a remark of my wife's. It ran: 'Couldn't we afford a dog, dear? It'd keep me company while you're in town chasing around with those doxies of yours.' Quick to humour a woman's whim, I drove the poor little soul to a roadside kennel that was closing out a job lot of pets. I soon found the ideal companion for her, a ten-cent turtle bearing the legend, 'Greetings from Savin Rock', but the willful creature must begin haggling over a chow with the proprietor, a shifty freebooter with only one eye. He could see well enough out of the other, however, to distinguish the bulge of my wallet, toward which he swung constantly, like the needle of a compass.

'You don't find them dogs every day', he told us confidentially, 'That pup was stolen from one of the finest homes in Germantown.' Aware that any show of feeling would increase the price, my wife cunningly betrayed her indifference by cradling the animal in her arms and covering his muzzle with kisses. The ruse worked, and we got him for only ninety dollars, less than the average man spends a month on Gutenberg Bibles.

It took nearly an hour for Wang's initial shyness to wear off. The last of it disappeared at the general store as motherly old Mrs Sigafoos bent over him to coo an endearment. With a sibilant hiss, he tore the fichu from her blouse and she fell into a display of fig bars. A hearty laugh and a dizzying bribe quickly restored good spirits, and we set off for home. En route, we stopped briefly at the villa of an artist neighbor for a cup of hot milk and grenadine. The door was opened by Mrs van Gogh, modishly clad in a new hostess gown for the occasion, bearing a Siamese cat in her arms. Wang joyfully blew battle stations, and Grimalkin, employing his mistress as a Jacob's ladder, hastily went topside and lodged in her coiffure. Over the iodine and gauze we all became fast friends, and I even bought a dry point from them which I needed like a hole in the head. My wife still insists I kept referring to it as a blue point, but of course she was somewhat unnerved.

For the next two days you never would have known there was a dog on the place, apart from an occasional stifled cry as Wang's teeth closed on a child. His daily routine was almost Spartan: in the morning a rapid round of the local garbage piles, at noon a casual lunch off two or three stray pullets, and toward sundown a vigorous uprooting of our shrubs. Thanks to this rigid discipline, he was trained to razor edge for his farewell performance. The setting was the porch and his co-star a schnauzer imported by a fair weekend guest. In the heat of the struggle, milady felt it best to thrust her foot between the actors. Wang, ever a boy with a sweet tooth, started stuffing himself, and it required a spirited massage with a bone-handled umbrella to distract the glutton. The hushed calm that ensued was broken only by the crackle of a crisp bank note and a deep sigh.

I traded Wang for a collie who brought home skunks, and turned Laddie Boy in for a Kerry who ate maids. At last, in desperation, I bought a bloodhound, a timid thing with great gentle eyes like a fawn. The man swore she was barely able to walk, much less attack anybody. A fortnight later, she knocked down a state trooper, stole his pistol, and held up a cigar store in Doylestown. And if you don't believe me, ask her brother. He's working for the Bureau of Internal Revenue.

From: *Acres and Pains*, by S. J. Perelman

There are certain phrases from the work of S. J. Perelman which seem like an everlasting source of energy, incapable of decay. I think of the unappealing little girl Leonie whose lips 'would melt the glue out of a revolving bookcase' and my bark of laughter is as though I had touched something live, as though the words themselves had given me an electric shock. This same effect – as if Perelman's access to the galvanic power of language were curiously independent of the meaning it carries – I find in his description of the film star's library which contained 'the cream of the world's great abridgements' or when his first sentence begins, 'We had dined famously off a charmburger ...' Mr Follansbee the bank manager has a smile that is 'reminiscent of a cheese blintz freshly fried in butter' and later opens his mouth to reveal 'four rows of teeth, like a basking shark'. And Philomene the coloured cook is 'built somewhat on the order of Lois de Fee, the lady bouncer. She had the rippling muscles of a panther, the stolidity of a water-buffalo, and the lazy insolence of a shoe salesman'.

Nonchalant irony, surreal disdain, is the very accent of Perelman's humour, but his command of the language itself borders on the alchemical. In the piece above – taken from a collection called Acres and Pains, a series of jeremiads on country-cottage dwelling 'through whose pages' as Perelman himself wrote 're-sound the cheep of the junco, the croak of bullfrogs, and the wail of the oppidan who has been taken to the cleaners' – the crisp cerebral snap of the words is an invitation to grown-up laughter.

THE MOST REVEREND AND RT HON. ROBERT RUNCIE
ARCHBISHOP OF CANTERBURY

Nobody has suffered more from low spirits than I have done, so I feel for you. 1. Live as well and drink as much wine as you dare. 2. Go into the shower-bath with a small quantity of water at a temperature low enough to give you a *slight sensation of cold* – 75 or 80°. 3. Amusing books. 4. Short views of human life not farther than dinner or tea. 5. Be as busy as you can. 6. See as much as you can of those friends who respect and like you; 7. and of those acquaintance who amuse you. 8. Make no secret of low spirits to your friends but talk to them fully: they are always the worse for dignified concealment. 9. Attend to the effects tea and coffee produce upon you. 10. Compare your lot with that of other people. 11. Don't expect too much of human life, a sorry business at the best. 12. Avoid poetry, dramatic representations (except comedy), music, serious novels, melancholy sentimental people, and everything likely to excite feeling or emotion not ending in active benevolence. 13. Do good and endeavour to please everybody of every degree. 14. Be as much as you can in the open air without fatigue. 15. Make the room where you commonly sit gay and pleasant. 16. Struggle by little and little against idleness. 17. Don't be too severe upon yourself, or underrate yourself, but do yourself justice. 18. Keep good blazing fires. 19. Be firm and constant in the exercise of rational religion. 20. Believe me dear Lady Georgiana very truly yours, Sydney Smith.

From: a letter to Lady Georgiana Morpeth, by Sydney Smith, quoted in *Sydney Smith: a biography*, by Alan Bell

In dealing with this complex psychological condition, the robust common sense of a former age can still remind us of truths easily forgotten.

DAME CICELY SAUNDERS
O.B.E.
MEDICAL DIRECTOR OF ST CHRISTOPHER'S HOSPICE

Thibault was too happy for speech. He was busy unroping the little barrel, and Abelard had risen, the segment of cheese in his hand, to reach down their drinking-horns from the wall, when both men suddenly stood still.

'My God,' said Thibault, 'what's that?'

From somewhere near them in the woods a cry had risen, a thin cry, of such intolerable anguish that Abelard turned dizzy on his feet, and caught at the wall.

'It's a child's voice,' he said. 'O God, are they at a child?'

Thibault had gone outside. The cry came again, making the twilight and the firelit hearth a mockery.

'A rabbit,' said Thibault. He listened. 'There's nothing worrying it. It'll be in a trap. Hugh told me he was putting them down. Christ!' The scream came yet again.

Abelard was beside him, and the two plunged down the bank.

'Down by the river,' said Thibault. 'I saw them playing, God help them, when I was coming home. You know the way they go demented with fun in the evenings. It will have been drumming with its hind paws to itself and brought down the trap.'

Abelard went on, hardly listening. 'O God,' he was muttering. 'Let it die quickly.'

But the cry came yet again. On the right, this time. He plunged through a thicket of hornbeam.

'Watch out,' said Thibault, thrusting past him. 'The trap might take the hand off you.'

The rabbit stopped shrieking when they stooped over it, either from exhaustion, or in some last extremity of fear. Thibault held the teeth of the trap apart, and Abelard gathered up the little creature in his hands. It lay for a moment breathing quickly, then in some blind recognition of the kindness that had met it at the last, the small head thrust and nestled against his arm, and it died.

It was that last confiding thrust that broke Abelard's heart.

He looked down at the little draggled body, his mouth shaking. 'Thibault,' he said, 'do you think there is a God at all? Whatever has come to me, I earned it. But what did this one do?'

Thibault nodded.

'I know,' he said. 'Only – I think God is in it too.'

Abelard looked up sharply.

'In it? Do you mean that it makes Him suffer, the way it does us?'

Again Thibault nodded.

'Then why doesn't he stop it?'

'I don't know,' said Thibault. 'Unless – unless it's like the Prodigal Son. I suppose the father could have kept him at home against his will. But what would have been the use? All this,' he stroked the limp body, 'is because of us. But all the time God suffers. More than we do.'

'Thibault, when did you think of all this?'

Thibault's face stiffened. 'It was that night,' he said, his voice strangled. 'The things we did to – to poor Guibert. He——' Thibault stopped. 'I could not sleep for nights and nights. And then I saw that God suffered too. And I thought I would like to be a priest.'

'Thibault, do you mean Calvary?'

Thibault shook his head. 'That was only a piece of it – the piece that we saw – in time. Like that.' He pointed to a fallen tree beside them, sawn through the middle. 'That dark ring there, it goes up and down the whole length of the tree. But you only see it where it is cut across. That is what Christ's life was; the bit of God that we saw. And we think God is like that, because Christ was like that, kind, and forgiving sins and healing people. We think God is like that for ever, because it happened once, with Christ. But not the pain. Not the agony at the last. We think that stopped.'

Abelard looked at him, the blunt nose and the wide mouth, the honest troubled eyes. He could have knelt before him.

'Then, Thibault,' he said slowly, 'you think that all this,' he looked down at the little quiet body in his arms, 'all the pain of the world, was Christ's cross?'

'God's cross,' said Thibault. 'And it goes on.'

'The Patripassian heresy,' muttered Abelard mechanically. 'But, oh God, if it were true. Thibault, it must be. At least, there is something at the back of it that is true. And if we could find it – it would bring back the whole world.'

'I couldn't ever rightly explain it,' said Thibault. 'But you could, if you would think it out.' He reached out his hand, and stroked the long ears. 'Old lop-ears,' he said. 'Maybe this is why he died. Come and have your supper, Master Peter. We'll bury him somewhere near the oratory. In holy ground.'

From: *Peter Abelard*, by Helen Waddell

I believe that the message of this episode is something I feel is sadly often missed in a lot of teaching about suffering.

PAUL SCOFIELD

ACTOR

And this is how I see the East.

I have seen its secret places and looked into its very soul; but now I see it always from a small boat, a high outline of mountains, blue and afar in the morning; like faint mist at noon; a jagged wall of purple at sunset.

I have the feel of the oar in my hand, the vision of a scorching blue sea in my eyes.

And I see a bay, a wide bay, smooth as glass and polished like ice, shimmering in the dark.

A red light burns far off upon the gloom of the land, and the night is soft and warm. We drag at the oars with aching arms, and suddenly a puff of wind, a puff faint and tepid and laden with strange odours of blossoms, of aromatic wood, comes out of the still night – the first sigh of the East upon my face.

That I can never forget. It was impalpable and enslaving, like a charm, like a whispered promise of mysterious delight.

From: *Youth*, by Joseph Conrad

When at school and at the age of, I think, thirteen my class was invited by the English master to choose a piece of either poetry or prose from our current curriculum and read it out in front of the rest of the class. Our choice was thus from Julius Caesar, Twelfth Night, Tennyson's 'In Memoriam' and some other well-known poems that I have now forgotten. We also were studying Conrad's two stories 'Youth' and 'Gaspar Ruiz'. It's hard to know why I chose a piece of prose rather than the many poetic and dramatic passages that were to hand. But I did, and somehow fixed for ever my own predilection for seeking out the poetry which is implicit in beautiful prose. It was once said to me by a colleague that I spoke, as an actor, poetry as if it were prose, and prose as if it were poetry. A back-handed compliment perhaps and, whether or not true, it is a characteristic that can be traced directly back to that odd choice I made in 1933 or 4.

SIR PETER SCOTT C.B.E.

ARTIST AND ORNITHOLOGIST

Of all the Knights in Appledore
   The wisest was Sir Thomas Tom.
He multiplied as far as four,
   And knew what nine was taken from
To make eleven. He could write
A letter to another Knight.

No other Knight in all the land
   Could do the things which he could do.
Not only did he understand
   The way to polish swords, but knew
What remedy a Knight should seek
Whose armour had begun to squeak.

And if he didn't fight too much,
   It wasn't that he did not care
For blips and buffetings and such,
   But felt that it was hardly fair
To risk, by frequent injuries,
A brain as delicate as his.

His castle (Castle Tom) was set
   Conveniently on a hill;
And daily, when it wasn't wet,
   He paced the battlements until
Some smaller Knight who couldn't swim
Should reach the moat and challenge him.

Or sometimes feeling full of fight,
   He hurried out to scour the plain;
And, seeing some approaching Knight,
   He either hurried home again,
Or hid; and, when the foe was past,
Blew a triumphant trumpet-blast.

One day when good Sir Thomas Tom
   Was resting in a handy ditch,

The noises he was hiding from,
  Though very much the noises which
He'd always hidden from before,
Seemed somehow less ... Or was it more?

The trotting horse, the trumpet's blast,
  The whistling sword, the armour's squeak,
These, and especially the last,
  Had clattered by him all the week.
Was this the same, or was it not?
Something was different. But what?

Sir Thomas raised a cautious ear
  And listened as Sir Hugh went by,
And suddenly he seemed to hear
  (Or not to hear) the reason why
This stranger made a nicer sound
Than other Knights who lived around.

Sir Thomas watched the way he went –
  His rage was such he couldn't speak,
For years they'd called him down in Kent
  The Knight Whose Armour Didn't Squeak!
Yet here and now he looked upon
Another Knight whose squeak had gone.

He rushed to where his horse was tied;
  He spurred it to a rapid trot.
The only fear he felt inside
  About his enemy was not
'How sharp his sword?' 'How stout his heart?'
But 'Has he got too long a start?'

Sir Hugh was singing, hand on hip,
  When something sudden came along,
And caught him a terrific blip
  Right in the middle of his song.
'A thunderstorm!' he thought. 'Of course!'
And toppled gently off his horse.

Then said the good Sir Thomas Tom,
  Dismounting with a friendly air,
'Allow me to extract you from
  The heavy armour that you wear.
At times like these the bravest Knight
May find his armour much too tight.'

A hundred yards or so beyond
  The scene of brave Sir Hugh's defeat
Sir Thomas found a useful pond,
  And, careful not to wet his feet,
He brought the armour to the brink,
And flung it in ... and watched it sink.

So ever after, more and more,
  The men of Kent would proudly speak
Of Thomas Tom of Appledore,
  'The Knight Whose Armour Didn't Squeak.'
Whilst Hugh, the Knight who gave him best,
Squeaks just as badly as the rest.

'The Knight whose armour didn't squeak', from: *Now We Are Six*, by A. A. Milne

I have always enjoyed the works of A. A. Milne and many years ago committed to memory his poem in *Now we are Six* about Sir Thomas Tom of Appledore, the Knight whose armour didn't squeak.

When, long years later, my Knighthood appeared in the Honours List, among the congratulatory communications I received was a small parcel from a close friend containing a bottle of oil labelled 'For Armour'.

The poem does not seem to have dated at all, and I still regard it as one of Milne's most delightful works.

CLIVE SINCLAIR
INVENTOR

I know that I shall meet my fate
Somewhere among the clouds above;
Those that I fight I do not hate
Those that I guard I do not love;
My country is Kiltartan Cross,
My countrymen Kiltartan's poor,
No likely end could bring them loss
or leave them happier than before.
Nor law, nor duty bade me fight,
Nor public men, nor cheering crowds,
A lonely impulse of delight
Drove to this tumult in the clouds;
I balanced all, brought all to mind,
The years to come seemed waste of breath,
A waste of breath the years behind
In balance with this life, this death.

'An Irish Airman foresees His Death', from *The Wild Swans
at Coole*, by W. B. Yeats

To choose a poem by Yeats that is not of Love, Faith or Nature
must seem perverse, but of all that he wrote this has meant most
to me. It is a poem of despair but of dignity too, and of the will.

It is sad, as Yeats so often is, but optimism underlies it. There
is a victory of the spirit in enjoying death when nothing else offers
the prospect of enjoyment.

But above all this is the rarely expressed feeling of an individual
acting with supreme independence.

When Yeats himself died, W. H. Auden wrote a poem in his
memory containing these lines:

> Earth: receive an honoured guest,
> William Yeats is laid to rest.
> Let the Irish vessel lie
> Empty of its poetry.

THE REV. THE LORD SOPER

METHODIST MINISTER

Prevent us, O Lord, in all our doings with thy most gracious favour, and further us with thy continual help: that in all our works, begun, continued, and ended in thee we may glorify thy Holy Name, and finally by thy mercy obtain everlasting life; through Jesus Christ our Lord.

From: *The Book of Common Prayer*

This is a magnificent piece of Elizabethan prose in which the majority of the words are Anglo-Saxon instead of Latin, and is none the worse for that.

The passage is all the more attractive because of the word 'Prevent' with which the prayer beings. The mind is immediately alerted to the need to understand the words of the Collect and not merely to recognise them. 'Prevent' of course means 'go before' and not 'put a stop to'.

Familiarity with language often breeds contempt for its significance. I welcome the discipline of interpreting the word 'Prevent' as a challenge to pursue that discipline with all the words that follow.

Finally, the prayer is for me a superb expression of Christian vocation and pilgrimage. The more frequently I come to it, the more powerfully is that meaning brought home to me.

DELIA SMITH
COOKERY WRITER AND BROADCASTER

O Lord, you search me and you know me,
you know my resting and my rising,
you discern my purpose from afar.
You mark when I walk or lie down,
all my ways lie open to you.

Before ever a word is on my tongue
you know it, O Lord, through and through.
Behind and before you besiege me,
your hand ever laid upon me.
Too wonderful for me, this knowledge,
too high, beyond my reach.

O where can I go from your spirit,
or where can I flee from your face?
If I climb the heavens, you are there.
If I lie in the grave, you are there.

If I take the wings of the dawn
and dwell at the sea's furthest end,
even there your hand would lead me,
your right hand would hold me fast.

If I say: 'Let the darkness hide me
and the light around me be night.'
even darkness is not dark for you
and the night is as clear as the day.

For it was you who created my being,
knit me together in my mother's womb.
I thank you for the wonder of my being,
for the wonders of all your creation.

Already you knew my soul,
my body held no secret from you
when I was being fashioned in secret
and moulded in the depths of the earth.

Your eyes saw all my actions,
they were all of them written in your book;
every one of my days was decreed
before one of them came into being.

To me, how mysterious your thoughts,
the sum of them not to be numbered;
If I count them, they are more than the sand;
to finish, I must be eternal, like you.

O search me, God, and know my heart,
O test me and know my thoughts.
See that I follow not the wrong path
and lead me in the path of life eternal.

Extract from Psalm 139, in: *The Psalms; a New Translation by The Grail*

I think the best prayer book that has ever been written is the book of psalms for anyone who has difficulty in prayer. They need only turn to the psalms to find something that will express exactly how they are feeling. The whole gamut of human emotions is written into the psalms.

It would be very hard for me to say which was my *most* favourite psalm. Psalm 139 is definitely one of my favourites, I feel that with prayers as rich as these, the only way to read them is very slowly and very quietly, reflecting on each line.

This is a self-affirming prayer, which helps the reader to grasp just how close they are to God and, more important, just how close He is to them.

GEOFFREY D. SMITH

HORTICULTURALIST, WRITER AND BROADCASTER

Here was the spring, at the foot of a perpendicular rock, moss-grown low down, and overrun with creeping ivy higher. Green thorn bushes filled the chinks and made a wall to the well, and the long narrow hart's-tongue streaked the face of the cliff. Behind the thick thorns hid the course of the streamlet, in front rose the solid rock, upon the right hand the sward came to the edge – it shook every now and then as the horses in the shade of the elms stamped their feet – on the left hand the ears of wheat peered over the verge. A rocky cell in concentrated silence of green things. Now and again a finch, a starling, or a sparrow would come meaning to drink – athirst from the meadow or the corn field – and start and almost entangle their wings in the bushes, so completely astonished that anyone should be there. The spring rises in a hollow under the rock imperceptibly, and without bubble or sound. The fine sand of the shallow basin is undisturbed – no tiny water volcano pushes up a dome of particles. Nor is there any crevice in the stone, but the basin is always full and always running over. As it slips from the brim a gleam of sunshine falls through the boughs and meets it. To this cell I used to come once now and then on a summer's day, tempted, perhaps, like the finches, by the sweet cool water, but drawn also by a feeling that could not be analysed. Stooping, I lifted the water in the hollow of my hand – carefully, lest the sand might be disturbed – and the sunlight gleamed on it as it slipped through my fingers. Alone in the green-roofed cave, alone with the sunlight and the pure water, there was a sense of something more than these. The water was more to me than water, and the sun than sun. The gleaming rays of the water in my palm held me for a moment, the touch of the water gave me something from itself. A moment, and the gleam was gone, the water flowed away, but I had had them. Beside the physical water and physical light I had received from them their beauty; they had communicated to me this silent mystery. The pure and beautiful water, the pure, clear, and beautiful light, each had given me something of their truth.

So many times I came to it, toiling up the long and shadowless hill in burning sunshine, often carrying a vessel to take some of it home with me. There was a brook, indeed; but this was different, it was the spring; it was taken home as a beautiful flower might be brought. It is not the physical water, it is the sense or feeling that it conveys. Nor is it the physical sunshine; it is the sense of inexpressible beauty which it brings with it. Of such I still drink, and hope to do so still deeper.

From: *The Life of the Fields*, by Richard Jefferies

There was no problem choosing the piece of writing, it had to be something written by Richard Jefferies.

I first read *The Life of the Fields* in my late teens, and it was as if someone had put into words my own sense of communion with the countryside.

There are other authors who speak a similar language to Jefferies as if they, too, explored what seems to be a further level of consciousness. Adrian Bell, J. H. B. Peel, and W. H. Hudson can feel, and what is more translate the emotion into words which express their intense delight in what Jefferies himself describes as 'the beauty and the delight of our woods and meadows. Green leaves and grass, and sunshine, blue skies and sparkle of the brook'. To them the natural countryside is more than just a pleasant backcloth to other activities, it is life itself. All in their way must be pronounced mystics, paying court to nature's illustrations yet discovering a satisfaction in the countryside which finds record in their essays.

RT HON. DAVID STEEL M.P.
LEADER OF THE LIBERAL PARTY

'What's this gen'ral election they keep talkin' about?' said Ginger. He directed the question at Henry because Henry had a reputation for universal knowledge, but he wasn't really interested. The general election was just a grown-up topic of conversation like the weather and the price of petrol, and so he took for granted that it must be as dull as any other grown-up topic of conversation.

'The general election means choosin' people to rule the country,' said Henry. 'There's four sorts of people tryin' to get to be rulers. They all want to make things better, but they want to make 'em better in different ways. There's Conservatives an' they want to make things better by keepin' 'em jus' like what they are now. An' there's Lib'rals an' they want to make things better by alterin' them jus' a bit, but not so's anyone'd notice, an' there's Socialists, an' they want to make things better by taking everyone's money off 'em an' there's Communists an' they want to make things better by killin' everyone but themselves.'

'I'm goin' to be one of them,' said Ginger promptly, 'they sound more excitin' than the others.' 'Well, they get everyone they can to vote for them,' went on Henry patiently, 'and the ones that gets the most votes win and their head man's called Prime Min'ster'. 'I say,' said Ginger excitedly, 'there's just four of us. Let's be them an' have one. I've bagged bein' the one that wants to kill everyone.'

'Let's get it settled,' said William. 'I'm bein' the Conservative, an' Ginger the Communist. Then there's the Socialist that wants to take other people's money off them –.' 'I'll be that,' put in Henry hastily.

'You'll have to be the Lib'ral, then,' said William to Douglas.

'I don't care,' said Douglas gloomily. 'I don't care what I am. I don't think it's goin' to be half such fun as Red Indians.'

The gathering in the old barn the next evening was larger than even the Outlaws had expected. The audience sat on the floor facing the Outlaws who sat on upturned packing-cases at one end. William stepped forward to explain the situation.

'Ladies an' Gent'men,' he began in his best platform manner, 'we're goin' to have a gen'ral election jus' the same as what grown-ups have. We're goin' to make speeches an' when we've finished you've all got to vote for us. Douglas is a Lib'ral an' Henry's a Socialist and Ginger's a Communist an' I'm a Conservative. Now we're all goin' to make speeches, startin' with Douglas.'

'Ladies an' Gentlemen,' said Douglas, 'I'm makin' this speech to ask you all to be Lib'rals same as what I am. Nearly all of you came to my birthday-party las' month an' if you don't vote Lib'rals I won't ask you again next year. My aunt's gotter parrot that talks, an' I'll let you come an' listen to it through the window when she's not there if you'll vote Lib'rals. I can't let you listen when she's there 'cause she doesn't like boys. I'll let you look at my rabbits too, an' I'll give you all a suck of rock if my aunt sends me a stick when she goes to Brighton same as she did last year.'

He sat down breathless. There were certainly the makings of a politician in Douglas. He didn't care what he promised.

William stood up. 'Now you ask him questions,' he said. 'Go on! Ask him questions! That's what they do when they've finished speakin'. It's called hecklin'.'

'It was a rotten party,' said a small boy in the front row bitterly, 'I gotter whistle out of a cracker an' it wouldn't whistle.'

'Well, that wasn't my fault,' said Douglas indignantly, 'I didn't make the crackers.'

'They must've been rotten crackers,' said the small boy.

'All right, you jolly well needn't come next year,' said Douglas heatedly.

'That's enough hecklin' about Liberalism,' said William . . . [After the others had spoken in turn] he announced, 'We'll have the voting now.'

'Hands up those who want to vote Lib'ral.' The audience remained motionless. 'Hands up those who want to vote Socialist.' The audience remained motionless. 'Hands up those who want to vote Communist.' The audience remained motionless. 'Hands up those who want to vote Conservative.' Every member of the audience immediately raised a hand.

'That's me,' said William complacently. 'I'm Prime Min'ster now. I'm goin' to rule the country.'

'What are you goin' to do for us first?' said the boy with red hair.

'Do for you?' repeated William indignantly, 'I'm not goin' to do anythin' for you. I'm goin' to *rule*.'

From: *William the Bad*, by Richmal Crompton

I think probably that during my school-days both in Kenya and in Edinburgh I read more for leisure than I have done since. I suppose so much of my work now involves reading for work that I don't get quite as much pleasure or time as I used to, for reading for leisure. But when I was a boy I read avidly. I read all the Arthur Ransome books, and all the Biggles books, and when I was younger, I read all the A. A. Milne, Winnie the Pooh books. And in particular – and this is what I've chosen from my childhood memories, I enjoyed the 'William' books. The piece I've chosen is from *William the Bad*, and it is where William and his gang, the Outlaws, decided to hold a General Election among themselves, with themselves as the characters.

I enjoyed reading this piece to my son Graham in bed a few years ago – whether he appreciated all the political side I don't know – but I still think it's a very good description of a General Election.

PROF. GEORGE STEINER
WRITER AND SCHOLAR

What thou lov'st well remains,
                              the rest is dross
What thou lov'st well shall not be reft from thee
What thou lov'st well is thy true heritage
Whose world, or mine or theirs
                              or is it of none?
First came the seen, then thus the palpable
            Elysium, though it were in the halls of hell,
What thou lovest well is thy true heritage
What thou lov'st well shall not be reft from thee

The ant's a centaur in his dragon world.
Pull down thy vanity, it is not man
Made courage, or made order, or made grace,
   Pull down thy vanity, I say pull down.
Learn of the green world what can be thy place
In scaled invention or true artistry,
Pull down thy vanity . . .

                  To have gathered from the air a live
                                          tradition
or from a fine old eye the unconquered flame
This is not vanity.
                  Here error is all in the not done,
all in the diffidence that faltered.

            From: 'Canto *LXXXI*', by Ezra Pound

These lines were written by Ezra Pound in his prison-cage at Pisa.
The half-crazed old man had committed ugly treason, broadcasting
vile pro-Fascist propaganga at American troops advancing up Italy.
He wrote the *Pisan Cantos* in more or less certain expectation of
a traitor's death. These lines constitute his *credo*. They sing, in-
comparably, of Pound's delight in antique beauty and the truth of
tradition; of his sense of man's unthinking arrogance and destruc-
tive impudence in the face of a natural world and of a natural

harmony which are not of his making. The tone is one of prophetic anguish. But the vital confidence of the poet hammers through: in the upbeat of those closing lines. This is a talismanic text; one to conduct one's life by. Yet it came out of 'the halls of Hell'. There is nothing simple or 'comforting' about the roots of great art and thought.

MARIKA HANBURY TENISON
JOURNALIST AND AUTHOR

And a woman who held a babe against her bosom said, Speak to us of Children.

And he said:

Your children are not your children.

They are the sons and daughters of Life's longing for itself.

They come through you but not from you,

And though they are with you yet they belong not to you.

You may give them your love but not your thoughts,

For they have their own thoughts.

You may house their bodies but not their souls,

For their souls dwell in the house of to-morrow, which you cannot visit, not even in your dreams.

You may strive to be like them, but seek not to make them like you.

For life goes not backward nor tarries with yesterday.

You are the bows from which your children as living arrows are sent forth.

The archer sees the mark upon the path of the infinite, and He bends you with His might that His arrows may go swift and far.

Let your bending in the Archer's hand be for gladness;

For even as He loves the arrow that flies, so He loves also the bow that is stable.

Then Almitra spoke again and said, And what of Marriage, master?

And he answered saying:

You were born together, and together you shall be for evermore.

You shall be together when the white wings of death scatter your days.

Aye, you shall be together even in the silent memory of God.

But let there be spaces in your togetherness.

And let the winds of the heavens dance between you.

Love one another, but make not a bond of love:
Let it rather be a moving sea between the shores of your souls.
Fill each other's cup but drink not from one cup.
Give one another of your bread but eat not from the same loaf.
Sing and dance together and be joyous, but let each one of you be alone,
Even as the strings of a lute are alone though they quiver with the same music.

Give your hearts, but not into each other's keeping.
For only the hand of Life can contain your hearts.
And stand together yet not too near together:
For the pillars of the temple stand apart,
And the oak tree and the cypress grow not in each other's shadow.

From: *The Prophet*, by Khalil Gibran

These poems were told me by a wonderful bishop whom I met when my husband and I were doing an expedition into the interior of Borneo by canoe, and we spent a month with Bishop Galvin who was without doubt one of the most Christian, kind and humorous people that it has ever been my fortune to meet. We were travelling in uncomfortable conditions staying with tribal groups in longhouses on the banks of the rivers. Bishop Galvin spoke many of the dialects and was dearly loved by these remote tribes. I learnt many things from him and have always been grateful to him for introducing me to these two poems which I feel form a good basis for the foundation of a good marriage and a happy relationship with ones children. Sadly six months after we left Borneo Bishop Galvin died.

RT HON. MARGARET THATCHER

THE PRIME MINISTER

Lord, thou knowest, better than I know myself that I am growing older, and will soon be old.

Keep me from getting talkative, and particularly from the fatal habit of thinking I must say something on every occasion.

Release me from the craving to try to straighten out everybody's affairs.

Make me thoughtful but not moody, helpful but not bossy.

With my vast store of wisdom it seems a pity not to use it all!

But thou knowest Lord that I want a few friends at the end.

Keep my mind from the endless recital of details.

Give me wings to get to the point.

Seal my lips on many aches and pains; they are increasing and my love of rehearsing them is becoming sweeter as the years go by.

Teach me the glorious lesson that occasionally it is possible that I may be mistaken.

Keep me reasonably sweet.

I do not want to be a saint – some of them are hard to live with – but a sour old man or woman is one of the works of the devil.

From: *The Bridge of Love, An Anthology of Hope*, edited by Elizabeth Bassett

The prayer I have chosen has always seemed to me to express in beautifully simple language thoughts which can only convey great insight to anyone who reads it.

R. S. THOMAS

POET

When into air had partially dissolved
That vision, given to spirits of the night
And three chance human wanderers, in calm thought
Reflected, it appeared to me the type
Of a majestic intellect, its acts
And its possessions, what it has and craves,
What in itself it is, and would become.
There I beheld the emblem of a mind
That feeds upon infinity, that broods
Over the dark abyss, intent to hear
Its voices issuing forth to silent light
In one continuous stream; a mind sustained
By recognitions of transcendent power,
In sense conducting to ideal form,
In soul of more than mortal privilege.
One function above all of such a mind
Had Nature shadowed there, by putting forth,
Mid circumstances awful and sublime,
That mutual domination which she loves
To exert upon the face of outward things,
So moulded, joined, abstracted, so endowed
With interchangeable supremacy,
That men, least sensitive, see, hear, perceive,
And cannot choose but feel. The power, which all
Acknowledge when thus moved, which Nature thus
To bodily sense exhibits, is the express
Resemblance of that glorious faculty
That higher minds bear with them as their own.
This is the very spirit in which they deal
With the whole compass of the universe:
They from their native selves can send abroad
Kindred mutations; for themselves create
A like existence; and, when'er it dawns
Created for them, catch it, or are caught
By its inevitable mastery

Like angels stopped upon the wing by sound
Of harmony from Heaven's remotest spheres.

From: *The Prelude*, Book Fourteenth, by William
Wordsworth

This is a passage to which I turn periodically as a corrective of a too
easy domestication of the Deity. In the increasingly humanistic
climate of to-day, it is well to remember that there are areas of life
which will remain probably for ever beyond the range of mortal
understanding and control. It is worth noting, too, that Wordsworth, writing over one hundred and fifty years ago, manages, as
all great writers do, to be surprisingly contemporary.

JOHN TIMPSON
BROADCASTER

The life that I have is
    all that I have,
And the life that I have
    is yours.
The love that I have
    of the life that I have
Is yours and yours
    and yours.

A sleep I shall have
A rest I shall have,
Yet death will be but
    a pause.
For the peace of my years
    in the long green grass
Will be yours and yours
    and yours.

Leo Marks

I came upon this, of all unlikely places, in the programme pages of
Radio Times, while I was checking to see if I was still employed
during the coming week ... It's so simply written, but it reads
beautifully. If I were a writer of love poems, I'd wish I'd written
that.

BARRY TOOK
BROADCASTER

For nowhere else but in England's capital are there spires like those tapering silver arrows of English stone, shell encrusted, sea worn, glittering in the sunlight with ten thousand sparkles of tiny diamonds. English churches built of English stone by an Englishman, a kindly poetical man, full of laughter, they were raised for the English people to follow their faith, not torn, like the great cathedrals, by violence and theft from Rome.

Another kindly man, a poet full of laughter, an Englishman, has written somewhere:

> Sir Christopher came to the field of the fire
> And graced it with spire
> And nave and choir,
> Careful column and carven tire,
> That the ships coming up from the sea
> Should hail where the Wards from Ludgate fall
> A coronal cluster of steeples tall,
> All Hallows, Barking, and by the Wall,
> St Bride, St Swithin,
> St Catherine Colman,
> St Margaret Pattens,
> St Mary le Bow,
> St Nicholas Cole Abbey,
> St Alban, Wood Street,
> St Magnus the Martyr,
> St Edmund the King,
> Whose names like a chime so sweetly call,
> And high over all
> The Cross and the Ball
> On the Riding Redoubtable Dome of Paul.

From: *England Their England*, by A. G. MacDonell

The piece I've chosen comes from A. G. Macdonell's book, England Their England, but no, it's not the description of the cricket match played at Fordenden by a team of thirties literati versus the local eleven. That chapter is renowned among all who cherish laughter, and rightly so, as it is one of the best pieces of sustained humour in print. [See Brian Johnston's Choice! – Editors.].

The moment of England Their England I have chosen is from a later chapter which describes how Donald Cameron, the young Scottish hero of the book, spends his Saturday afternoons ('for they are usually closed on Sundays') visiting the Churches in the city of London.

I find it impossible to read it without a tingle running through me – the same tingle I felt when I first read the book forty years ago.

P. L. TRAVERS O.B.E.
AUTHOR

Art thou poor, yet hast thou golden slumbers?
    O sweet content!
  Art thou rich, yet is thy mind perplexéd?
    O punishment!
  Dost thou laugh to see how fools are vexéd
To add to golden numbers golden numbers?
    O sweet content! O sweet, O sweet content!
  Work apace, apace, apace, apace;
  Honest labour bears a lovely face;
  Then hey nonny nonny – hey nonny nonny!

Canst drink the waters of the crispéd spring?
    O sweet content!
  Swim'st thou in wealth, yet sink'st in thine own tears?
    O punishment!
  Then he that patiently want's burden bears,

  No burden bears, but is a king, a king!
    O sweet content! O sweet, O sweet content!
  Work apace, apace, apace, apace;
  Honest labour bears a lovely face;
  Then hey nonny nonny – hey nonny nonny!

'The Basket Maker's Song', from: *Patient Grissill*, by
Thomas Dekker

I have chosen this piece not only because it is one of my favourite poems but because it accepts life and praises work. Perhaps the two things are indistinguishable. For no matter how many talents a man is given, if he is denied the talent for work, he can make use of none of them. Where would Leonardo and Shakespeare have been without this plus, this extra grace?

And Dekker's Basket Maker clearly had it.

CHAD VARAH

FOUNDER OF THE SAMARITANS

Oft have I seen, at some cathedral door
A labourer, pausing in the dust and heat,
Lay down his burden, and with reverent feet
Enter, and cross himself, and on the floor
Kneel to repeat his Paternoster o'er.
Far off the noises of the world retreat;
The loud vociferations of the street
Become an indistinguishable roar.

So, as I enter here from day to day
And leave my burden at this minster gate,
Kneeling in prayer, and not ashamed to pray
The tumult of the time disconsolate
To inarticulate murmurs dies away,
While the eternal ages watch and wait.

First sonnet from: 'Divina Commedia', by Henry Wadsworth
Longfellow

Much have I travelled in the realms of gold,
And many goodly States and Kingdoms seen;
Round many western islands have I been
Which bards in fealty to Apollo hold.
Oft of one wide expanse had I been told
That deep-browed Homer ruled as his demesne;
Yet did I never breathe its pure serene
Til I heard Chapman speak out loud and bold;
Then felt I like some watcher of the skies
When a new planet swims into his ken;
Or like stout Cortez when with eagle eyes
He stared at the Pacific – and all his men
Looked at each other with a wild surmise
Silent, upon a peak in Darien.

'On first looking into Chapman's Homer', by John Keats

I have chosen two sonnets about the magic of books.

The definition of dysphasia must make those of us who derive most of our pleasure from 'reading and understanding others' words' grateful for what we have and fearful of losing it. As one who has enjoyed reading from his infancy, choosing from a hundred pieces jostling for selection was difficult, so I followed my first impulse and put together two of the sonnets read to me by my father when I was about 5 years old and which I haven't seen linked elsewhere. I have to admit that I am not an avid reader of either the *Divine Comedy* or Chapman's translation of Homer, but I appreciate the communication of enthusiasm and have revelled in many reviews of books I am unlikely to read. I think I could be eloquent about books which have enlarged me, such as James Branch Cabell's *Jurgen*, or C. S. Lewis's *The Great Divorce* and his trilogy of space fiction. I am glad poetry is being read more, because at its best it uses words with the precision I require as a scientist and the overtones and undertones and allusions and sometimes ecstasy which I seek as a Christian.

ARNOLD WESKER
PLAYWRIGHT

i
'A fragment of a plate dug up June 14th, '66'

The fragment of a plate
shows me a man:
almost myself I've thought him –
any rate
what he looks at
beneath his wide-brimmed hat,
is in a jagged corner
where I can
just see a fragment of an eye
beside a curl:
a woman's, I am almost sure of that.

I thought
about this shard
upon a walk
inside a wood, but caught
myself reflecting on a burl
dependant 'twixt their view –
it was a riddle
that I now discard
to ponder what they say but not in talk.

I sense that it reflects on my own life.
Is it bound up with that beyond recall?
Then trying to recall if ever I did sue
to some forgotten maid to be my wife,
a sleepy farm comes back, one which I went to
morning after morning, meeting there
a pink-cheeked maid,
so wistful, with dark hair.
But why? I did not woo her –
few words we ever said –
she so like a silent Summer brook.

Only now I hear the fragment state:
'Who wooed not was yet loved –
he missed the meaning –
the meaning that was hidden in her look.'

In fancy now I dwell upon her parish,
dreaming
how there was all I should have cherished,
and how a broken heart's a broken plate.
The fragment came from her plate of the set
mine never made,
having loved not
that sweet maid till now, too late.

I thought: what had been broken out of grief,
she salvaged later, when, with grief less showing,
but bitterness beginning in its stead,
she cast this to the plot I turned today,
so I should fathom long and after fret
not only over love I might have had,
but what she kept: the other fragments' secret,
the full pattern knowing.

ii
'Glances on a Bus'

'I seem to think we once met on a woodland path:
yes, through the skirting elms as I walked one Sabbath,
I saw you tripping down selions on the left rowen's swath.'
  'I am stared at,' glanced she.

'Verging the right angle of plough, I watched your swift
          searching
'twixt down swoops in ditch brews for what? Oh of course
          your deep stooping

and spurts I remember me now were in the sweet Spring!'
      'Who is he?' glanced she.

I thought: 'she plucks flowers in bursts for one who leaves
          soon,
and already she knows it is late in the afternoon.

Has she not yet her nosegay? Nor sees she the swarth of the
moon?
'Do I know him?' glanced she.

'As you entered the dream woodland path, how I wished I
could tell you
I feared your rapt coming on me would suddenly start you,
so deliberately turning away, I cast only a glance at you.'
'Those eyes,' glanced she.

'But blush on you, breathless blanch on you, primroses in
hand,
(how lovely the spell that you cast of an innocent land!)
I hold dear and would thank you for now, for its picture
will stand.'
'It's my stop,' glanced she.

'Primly she rose at her stop, also mine, thus to stress
I knew it *was* she. But remember *me*? Her glance then said
'Yes.
You are the man that I dream of lifting my dress
in the woods to deflower me.'

iii
'Jack and Jill'

No, Jack did never have his Jill
except in childhood
when the wild wood
rang with hornings to the hill,
Jill then Jack's Maid Marian,
Jack Jill's Robin, –
why that land,
Oh happy, happy, happy land,
of kingcup joys

and merry boys
with Jack the leader of their band,
should have passed away for good –
Jack packed away to maidless manhood,
Jill to pick a counterpane
of kingcups
of her childhood

in Robin Hoodless womanhood –
is not for Jill to understand.
Jill unmaidened and forlorn,
wed to some Sir Guy of Gisborne,
says often to her counterpane:
    'Life Oh you,
      ungallant you,
who have me here, whilst in my brain
still I'm far away with him,
my Robin Jack, mean you this whim,
    that when you kill
    both Jack and Jill,
    yours is the grace –
    Oh you who thrive
    on every man Jack –
    to give back
    that childhood place
    and only heaven
    to Jack then seven,
    Jill then five?'
Life answers. 'Yes,' whilst Jill is alive.

'What Jack Told Me', three poems by Roger Frith

Roger Frith was born at Wanstead, in Essex, on the 4th April,
1936. His father and mother were concert singers who later went
into service. In 1961 his father, who never recovered from his experiences in the First World War, died, and the loss, with tragic
paradox, lurched him into his first serious writings.

One of our strongest emotions is the one felt when we remember
time passing. The force of the emotion lies in the conflict and
diversity of feelings aroused: pleasure that there was happiness,
sadness that it has passed; satisfaction with what was achieved;
shame for the failures, and bitterness that they cannot be rectified;
remembered joy; regret for missed opportunities; the wistful
ache for lost innocence, and the heavier ache for 'all passion
spent'.

Poetry is to do with such an emotion, and these three parts to the
poem 'What Jack Told Me' – from Frith's second of three published books – seem to me to echo many of those feelings. And
they do so in a language that feels rural, archaic, yet is of now.

As though the poet is declaring he belongs to the main river of language and poetry, and has not ambled off into an ephemeral tributary.

KATHARINE WHITEHORN
JOURNALIST

The trend of our epoch up to this time has been consistently towards specialism and professionalism. We tend to have trained soldiers because they fight better, trained singers because they sing better, trained dancers because they dance better, specially instructed laughers because they laugh better, and so on and so on. The principle has been applied to law and politics by innumerable modern writers. Many Fabians have insisted that a greater part of our political work should be performed by experts. Many legalists have declared that the untrained jury should be altogether supplanted by the trained judge.

Now, if this world of ours were really what is called reasonable, I do not know that there would be any fault to find with this. But the true result of all experience and the true foundation of all religion is this. That the four or five things that it is most practically essential that a man should know, are all of them what people call paradoxes. That is to say, that though we all find them in life to be mere plain truths, yet we cannot easily state them in words without being guilty of seeming verbal contradictions. One of them, for instance, is the unimpeachable platitude that the man who finds most pleasure for himself is often the man who least hunts for it. Another is the paradox of courage; the fact that the way to avoid death is not to have too much aversion to it. Whoever is careless enough of his bones to climb some hopeless cliff above the tide may save his bones by that carelessness. Whoever will lose his life, the same shall save it; an entirely practical and prosaic statement.

Now, one of these four or five paradoxes which should be taught to every infant prattling at his mother's knee is the following: That the more a man looks at a thing, the less he can see it, and the more a man learns a thing the less he knows it. The Fabian argument of the expert, that the man who is trained should be the man who is trusted, would be absolutely unanswerable if it were really true that a man who studied a thing and practised it every day went on seeing more and more of its significance. But he does not. He goes on seeing less and less of its significance. In the same way, alas! we all go on every day, unless we are continually goading ourselves into gratitude and humility, seeing less and less of the significance of the sky or the stones.

Now, it is a terrible business to mark a man out for the vengeance of men. But it is a thing to which a man can grow accustomed, as he can to other terrible things; he can even grow accustomed to the sun. And the horrible thing about all legal officials, even the best, about all judges, magistrates, barristers, detectives, and policemen, is not that they are wicked (some of them are good), not that they are stupid (several of them are quite intelligent), it is simply that they have got used to it.

Strictly they do not see the prisoner in the dock; all they see is the usual man in the usual place. They do not see the awful court of judgment; they only see their own workshop. Therefore, the instinct of Christian civilisation has most wisely declared that into their judgments there shall upon every occasion be infused fresh blood and fresh thoughts from the streets. Men shall come in who can see the court and the crowd, and coarse faces of the policemen and the professional criminals, the wasted faces of the wastrels, the unreal faces of the gesticulating counsel, and see it all as one sees a new picture or a play hitherto unvisited.

Our civilisation has decided, and very justly decided, that determining the guilt or innocence of men is a thing too important to be trusted to trained men. It wishes for light upon that awful matter, it asks men who know no more law than I know, but who can feel the things that I felt in the jury box. When it wants a library catalogued, or the solar system discovered, or any trifle of that kind, it uses up its specialists. But when it wishes anything done which is really serious it collects twelve of the ordinary men standing round. The same thing was done, if I remember right, by the Founder of Christianity.

From: 'The Twelve Men', by G. K. Chesterton

I like this essay by G. K. Chesterton because it seems to me to say so succinctly things which have become more true since he died in 1936 and not less. The prose is vivid, of course, but when it really comes down to it there is nothing that improves the efforts of any writer more thoroughly than having something to say.

MARY WILSON
POET

Primroses, daffodils, jasmine and crocus,
  Pale chilly flowers of hesitant Spring
Gathered with catkins and new-budded branches;
  Set in a bowl by the window, they bring
Promise of poppies and daisies and roses –
All the bright tangle of full summer bloom;
  Scented like lilies, austere in their beauty,
Lighting with yellow my winter-dark room.

'The Flowers of Spring', from: *New Poems*, by Mary Wilson

YEVGENY YEVTUSHENKO

POET

With blood still dripping from its

                      warm and sticky beak,

Its neck dangling over a bucket's edge,

A goose lies rocking in a boat,

                  like an ingot

Of slightly tarnished silver.

There had been two of them flying above the Vilyúi.

The first had been brought down in flight

                    while the other,

Gliding low,

        risking his neck,

Hovers over the lake,

           cries over the forest:

'My dove-grey brother,

            we came into the world

Clamorously breaking through our shells,

But every morning

        mother and father

Fed you first,

      when it might have been me.

My dove-grey brother,

        you had this blue

            tinge,

Teasing the sky with a bold similarity.

I was darker,

     and the females desired

You more,

    when it might have been me.

My dove-grey brother,

       without fear for the return,

You and I flew away, over the seas,

But obnoxious geese from other lands surrounded

You first,

     when it might have been me.

My dove-grey brother,

        we were beaten and bowed.

Together we were lashed by the tempests,

But for some reason the water slid
More easily off *your* goose's back,
                        when it might have been mine.
My dove-grey brother,
                we frayed our feathers.
People will eat both of us by the fireside –
Perhaps because the struggle to be first
Devoured you,
                consumed me.
My dove-grey brother,
                        half our lives was a pecking match,
Not treasuring our brotherhood, our wings and our souls.
Was reliance really impossible –
I on you,
        and you on me?
My dove-grey brother,
                I beg at least for a pellet,
Curbing my envy too late;
But for my punishment people killed
You first,
        when it might have been me ...'

'Lament for a Brother', from: *The face behind the face*, by
Yevgeny Yevtushenko, translated by Simon Franklin and
Arthur Boyars

Envy is among the foulest and most terrible of human emotions.
Envy of somebody else's talent, of somebody else's success, of
somebody else's beauty, health or happiness. Envy which gnaws
at one's innards, like the fox-cub which chewed through the innards
of the young Spartan who hid it under his shirt. Not only
personal envy: social envy is equally hideous. And national envy
– it leads to war. Political envy. Envy is always self-destructive.
    Once, when travelling with friends on the river Vilyui in
Siberia, I killed one of a pair of geese which were flying overhead.
Its companion stayed above us for a whole day, screeching. This
protracted posthumous lament sounded almost like an apology for
past wrongs, as if, it occurred to me, the survivor had in life
felt envious of the goose which I had shot, and only now did he
realise the horrific injustice of his envy. Unfortunately we humans
are prone to the same error. We nurture envy of others, and we
appreciate them properly only when we lose them.

SUSANNAH YORK

ACTRESS

I sing of a maiden that is makeles;
King of all kings to her son she ches.
He came al so stille, there his moder was,
As dew in Aprille that falleth on the grass.
He came al so stille to his moder's bour,
As dew in Aprille that falleth on the flour.
He came al so stille, there his moder lay,
As dew in Aprille that falleth on the spray.
Moder and mayden was never none but she;
Well may such a lady Godde's moder be.

'Carol', Anon (fifteenth century)

It's an expression of wonder, as immediate as when it was
conceived – perhaps in the mouth of a peasant who stopped in his
tracks as he sowed, or of a woman scrubbing clothes at the river,
or of her son swinging his legs over the bank while he watched her –
it's April breaking over them all! An expression of that wonder we
used to feel so often as children and recognise now with longing;
sudden, joyful, uncomplicated by thought.

ACKNOWLEDGEMENTS

To George Allen and Unwin (Publishers) Ltd and the author for the extract from Brian Patten's *Grave Gossip*.

To George Allen and Unwin (Publishers) Ltd and the author's executors for the extracts from Bertrand Russell's *Sceptical Essays* and *The Autobiography of Bertrand Russell* (Vol. II).

To Barrie & Jenkins Ltd and the author's estate for the extract from *The Well of Loneliness* by Radclyffe Hall.

To Barrie & Jenkins Ltd and A. P. Watt Ltd for the extract from P. G. Wodehouse's *The Man With Two Left Feet*.

To Big Ben Music Ltd, Charter Film Music Ltd and the author for the poem by Leo Marks.

To Blackie & Son Ltd for the extract from *Westminster* by J. D. Carlton.

To the Bodley Head Ltd, the author and the author's agents, Laurence Pollinger Ltd for the extract from Graham Greene's *The Quiet American*.

To Marion Boyars Publishers Ltd and the author for the poem 'Lament for a Brother' by Yevgeny Yevtushenko in *The Face Behind the Face* translated by Simon Franklin and Arthur Boyars.

To James Brodie Ltd and the author's representatives for the extract from G. K. Chesterton's *Essays*.

To Jonathan Cape Ltd and the author for the extract from Brian Aldiss' *The Eighty Minute Hour*.

To Jonathan Cape Ltd, Curtis Brown Ltd and the author for the extract from *Arguments for Socialism* by Tony Benn M.P.

To Jonathan Cape Ltd and the author for the extract from *Conducted Tour* by Bernard Levin.

To Jonathan Cape Ltd and the author for 'Head Injury' from Roger McGough's *After the Merrymaking*.

To Jonathan Cape Ltd and the author's estate for the extract from Arthur Ransome's *Pigeon Post*.

To Jonathan Cape Ltd and the author for Henry Reed's 'Naming of Parts' from *A Map of Verona*.

Charles Causley's translation of Rimbaud's 'Le Dormeur du Val' appeared originally in *Encounter* and is reproduced by permission of the translator and his agents David Higham Associates Ltd.

To Chatto & Windus Ltd for two extracts from C. G. Cavafy's *Collected Poems* translated by Edmund Keely and Phillip Sherard.

247

To Chatto & Windus Ltd and the author's literary estate for the extract from Maurice O'Sullivan's *Twenty Years A-Growing*.

To Co-Evolution Quarterly of P.O. Box 428, Sausalito, Ca. 94966 USA, and the author, for 'Snake' by Anne Herbert.

To William Collins Sons & Co. Ltd, A. P. Watt Ltd and the Grail, England for Pslam 139 from *The Psalms; a New Translation*.

To Constable & Co. Ltd and the author for the extract from Helen Waddell's *Peter Abelard*.

For the edited extract from Richmal Crompton's *William the Bad* (Newnes) to A. P. Watt Ltd and Mrs Richmal C. Ashbee.

To J. M. Dent & Sons Ltd, the author's estate and David Higham Associates Ltd for the extracts from Dylan Thomas's *Collected Poems* and *Reminiscences of Childhood*.

To Dobson Books Ltd and the author for the extract from Robert Benchley's *One Minute Please*.

To Doubleday & Co. Inc. and the author for 'The Meadow Mouse' by Theodore Roethke.

The extract from 'Ash Wednesday' from *Collected Poems 1909–1962* by T. S. Eliot is reprinted by special permission of Faber & Faber Ltd and Mrs Eliot.

To Faber & Faber Ltd and the author for the extract from *The Inheritors* by William Golding.

To Faber & Faber Ltd and the author for the extract from Philip Larkin's *High Windows*.

To Faber & Faber Ltd and the author's executors for the extract from *The Collected Poems of Louis MacNeice*.

To Faber & Faber Ltd and the author's estate for the extracts from *The Complete Poems of Marianne Moore*.

'Edward Lear' by W. H. Auden is reprinted by permission of Faber & Faber Ltd from *Collected Poems*.

To Faber & Faber Ltd and the Trustees of the Ezra Pound Literary Property Trust for the extract from *The Cantos of Ezra Pound*.

To Faber & Faber Ltd and Myfanwy Thomas for 'Words' from *Collected Poems* by Edward Thomas.

To Roger Frith for 'What Jack Told Me' (privately printed).

'The Thieves' by Robert Graves from *Collected Poems* is reprinted by permission of the author and A. P. Watt Ltd.

To Guardian Newspapers Ltd and the author for the extract by John Maddox.

To Harper and Row Inc. and Farrar Straus and Giroux Inc. for the extract from *The Oriental Philosophers – An Introduction* by E. W. F. Tomlin.

To Heinemann Educational Books Ltd and Antony Hopkins for the extract from *The Nine Symphonies of Beethoven.*

To David Higham Associates Ltd and Mrs Pudney for the extract from John Pudney's *Collected Poems* (Putnam & Co.)

To the Hon. Neil Hogg for his poem 'Traveller's Song' from *The Zodiac* (privately printed).

To the Hutchinson Publishing Group Ltd and the author and translator for the extract from *Way Out in the Centre* by Amir Gilboa, translated by Dannie Abse.

To the Hutchinson Publishing Group Ltd, the author and her agent, Rupert Crew Ltd for the extract from *The Light of Love* by Barbara Cartland.

To the Hutchinson Publishing Group Ltd and the author for the poem 'The Flowers of Spring' from *New Poems* by Mary Wilson.

To London Magazine Editions and the author for the poem by Christopher Hope.

To the Longman Group Ltd and the author's estate for the extract from *Facts of the Faith* by Canon Scott Holland.

To Macmillan (Publishers) Ltd, David Higham Associates Ltd and the author for the extract from Charles Causley's *Collected Poems* 1951–1975.

To Macmillan (Publishers) Ltd and the author's estate for the extracts from A. G. MacDonnell's *England, Their England.*

To Macmillan (Publishers) Ltd for the extract from Rabindranath Tagore's *Gitanjali.*

To Macmillan (Publishers) Ltd, M. B. Yeats and Anne Yeats for the extract from W. B. Yeats' *Collected Poems.*

To Mencap and the author for the extract from *Tongue Tied* by Joey Deacon.

To Methuen (London) Ltd and the author's estate for the poem from *Now We Are Six* by A. A. Milne.

To Methuen (London) Ltd and the author for the extract from Harold Pinter's *A Night Out* taken from *A Slight Ache and Other Plays.*

For the poems by Adrian Mitchell, to the author and *Peace News.*

For the extract from Robert Muldoon's *My Way* to the author.

To John Murray (Publishers) Ltd and the author for the extract from Sir John Betjeman's *Collected Poems.*

To The National Trust and A. P. Watt Ltd for two poems by Rudyard Kipling from *The Definitive Edition of Rudyard Kipling's Verse* (Macmillan).

To Penguin Books Ltd and the translator for an extract from Xenophon's *The Persian Expedition* translated by Rex Warner (Penguin Classics 1949 pp. 164–5) Copyright © Rex Warner 1949.

To Peter Masric Literistic Inc. for the extract from *Acres and Pains* by S. J. Perelman.

To A. D. Peters & Co. Ltd and the author's estate for the extract from *Scoop* by Evelyn Waugh.

To Phoenix House Ltd and the author's estate for the extract from A. J. Liebling's *The Sweet Science*.

To Random House Inc. and the author for the poem from Maya Angelou's *And Still I Rise*.

To Robson Books Ltd and the author for the poem 'Shy Children' from David Kossoff's *You Have a Minute, Lord?*

To Routledge and Kegan Paul Ltd for the extract from C. G. Jung's *Psychology and Religion*.

To Martin Secker and Warburg Ltd for 'The Fairy Ring' from Andrew Young's *Complete Poems*.

To N. F. Simpson for the poem 'One of Our St Bernard Dogs is Missing'.

To the Society of Authors as Literary Representative of the estate of John Masefield for 'A Creed'.

To Souvenir Press Ltd for the extract from Knut Hamsun's *The Growth of the Soil*.

To Sweet & Maxwell Ltd and the author for the extract from Lord Denning's *Freedom Under the Law*.

The extract from *All Men Are Brothers* by Mahatma Gandhi © Unesco 1958 is reproduced by permission of Unesco.

To Virago Ltd and the author's estate for the extract from *Novel on Yellow Paper* (Virago Press) by Stevie Smith.

To George Weidenfeld & Nicolson Ltd and the author for the extract from *The Needle's Eye* by Margaret Drabble.

To Gordon Zahn and Irvington Publications Inc. for the extract from *In Solitary Witness*.

INDEX OF AUTHORS